POPULATION CONTROL— or RACE TO OBLIVION?

Overpopulation is now the dominant problem in all our personal, national, and international planning.

No one can do rational personal planning, nor can public policy be resolved in any area unless one first takes into account the population bomb.

Schools, politicians, and mass media only touch the edge of the major problem.

Paul R. Ehrlich, a qualified scientist, clearly describes the dimensions of the crisis in all its aspects—air, food, water, birth control, death control, our total environment—and provides a realistic evaluation of the remaining options.

"Man marks the earth with ruin . . .
Our air is noxious, our wildlife is vanishing,
Even the oceans are threatened."

THE FRAIL OCEAN
Wesley Marx

"A fascinating and important book. The obvious comparison is with Rachel Carson's *Silent Spring*, and I can only hope Mr. Marx's book will be as widely read, and have a comparable impact." —*New York Times*
A Sierra Club/Ballantine Book   95¢

MOMENT IN THE SUN
Robert and Leona Train Rienow

"A very important book . . . we've been told for some years now that the wide open spaces are getting narrower all the time. The authors of this book lay it right on the line . . . after reading this sane and humane book, one wants to plead with everybody to keep aware, and not regard these things as part of some inevitable black comedy."—*Harper's*
"Man's accelerating destruction of his own habitat has never been so dramatically presented . . . a blockbuster of a book."
—*San Francisco Chronicle*
A Sierra Club/Ballantine Book   95¢

S/S/T AND SONIC BOOM HANDBOOK
William A. Shurcliff

A documented source book on the supersonic transport planes (SST's) now being developed by the U. S. at a starting cost of $600 million. This is the program approved by President Nixon despite the negative recommendations of his own investigative committee. This book demonstrates that the SST is an incredible, unnecessary insult to the living environment, dangerous and destructive to animals and human alike. It tells what you can do to stop this program in time and exactly why the supersonic transport *must* be stopped—now!
A Ballantine/Friends of the Earth Book   95¢

The words "The Population Bomb," selected as the title for this book, were first used in 1954 on the cover of a pamphlet issued by the Hugh Moore Fund. Annual editions of the pamphlet have been issued and widely distributed totaling over two million copies. The terms "population bomb" and "population explosion" which are now in general circulation were first used in this pamphlet.

THE
POPULATION
BOMB

Dr. Paul R. Ehrlich

BALLANTINE BOOKS   •   NEW YORK
An Intext Publisher

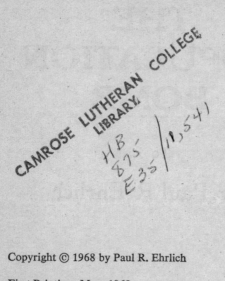

First Printing: May, 1968
Second Printing: August, 1968
Third Printing: August, 1968
Fourth Printing: January, 1969
Fifth Printing: March, 1969
Sixth Printing: June, 1969
Seventh Printing: September, 1969
Eighth Printing: October, 1969
Ninth Printing: November, 1969
Tenth Printing: December, 1969
Eleventh Printing: January, 1970
Twelfth Printing: January, 1970
Thirteenth Printing: February, 1970

PRINTED IN THE UNITED STATES OF AMERICA

BALLANTINE BOOKS, INC.
101 Fifth Avenue, New York, New York 10003

Sierra Club
220 Bush Street
San Francisco, Calif. 94104

To Lisa

TABLE OF CONTENTS

PROLOGUE

The battle to feed all of humanity is over. In the 1970's the world will undergo famines—hundreds of millions of people are going to starve to death in spite of any crash programs embarked upon now. At this late date nothing can prevent a substantial increase in the world death rate, although many lives could be saved through dramatic programs to "stretch" the carrying capacity of the earth by increasing food production. But these programs will only provide a stay of execution unless they are accompanied by determined and successful efforts at population control. Population control is the conscious regulation of the numbers of human beings to meet the needs, not just of individual families, but of society as a whole.

Nothing could be more misleading to our children than our present affluent society. They will inherit a totally different world, a world in which the standards, politics, and economics of the 1960's are dead. As the most powerful nation in the world today, *and its largest consumer,* the United States cannot stand isolated. We are today involved in the events leading to famine; tomorrow we may be destroyed by its consequences.

Our position requires that we take immediate action at home and promote effective action worldwide. We must have population control at home, hopefully through a system of incentives and penalties, but by compulsion if voluntary methods fail. We must use our political power to push other countries into programs which combine agricultural development and population control. And while this is being done we must take action to reverse the deterioration of our environment before population pressure permanently ruins our planet. The birth rate must be brought into balance with the death rate or mankind will breed itself into oblivion. We can no longer afford merely to treat the symptoms of the cancer of population growth; the cancer itself must be cut out. Population control is the only answer.

FOREWORD

Man can undo himself with no other force than his own brutality. It is a new brutality, coming swiftly at a time when, as Loren Eiseley says, "the need is for a gentler race. But the hand that hefted the axe against the ice, the tiger, and the bear now fondles the machine gun as lovingly."

The roots of the new brutality, it will become clear from *The Population Bomb,* are in the lack of population control. There is, we must hope and predict, a chance to exert control in time. We would like to predict that organizations which, like the Sierra Club, have been much too calm about the ultimate threat to mankind, will awaken themselves and others, and awaken them with an urgency that will be necessary to fulfillment of the prediction that mankind will survive.

It was only twelve years ago that we even suggested, in any Sierra Club publication, that uncontrolled population was a menace. We went far enough to write: "People are recognizing that we cannot forever continue to multiply and subdue the earth without losing our standard of life and the natural beauty that must be part of it....These are the years of decision— the decision of men to stay the flood of man."

In the next two years we worried about the battle of man versus his own numbers and were concerned that growth itself was growing and were not joyful about the imminence of California's outstripping New York.

It was Professor Raymond Cowles who shook us loose with a provocative address before a Sierra Club conference, "The Meaning of Wilderness to Science."

What in the late fifties had seemed heretical soon was not so. For the complaints that I had received about mentioning population problems in early speeches, there were more vociferous complaints if I forgot to mention the big problem. In just two or three years it became possible to question growth, to suggest that DNA was greater than GNP, to predict that man had enough genius to require that science and technology be put to good purpose. He could limit his numbers. He could limit his heretofore unslackened appetite for destroying wilderness. He could go back over the nine-tenths or so of the earth that had already felt his touch, sometimes a gentle touch but too often brutal, and do better where he had been. He could start with Manhattan, or Los Angeles.

Whatever resources the wilderness still held would not sustain him in his old habits of growing and reaching without limits. Wilderness could, however, provide answers for questions he had not yet learned how to ask. He could predict that the day of creation was not over, that there would be wiser men, and they would thank him for leaving the source of those answers. Wilderness would remain part of his geography of hope, as Wallace Stegner put it, and could, merely because wilderness endured on the planet, prevent man's world from becoming a cage.

The good predictions could be entertained—the notion of predicting a more and more desirable future, not just a more and more crowded one.

DAVID BROWER

CHAPTER 1

THE PROBLEM

I have understood the population explosion intellectually for a long time. I came to understand it emotionally one stinking hot night in Delhi a couple of years ago. My wife and daughter and I were returning to our hotel in an ancient taxi. The seats were hopping with fleas. The only functional gear was third. As we crawled through the city, we entered a crowded slum area. The temperature was well over 100, and the air was a haze of dust and smoke. The streets seemed alive with people. People eating, people washing, people sleeping. People visiting, arguing, and screaming. People thrusting their hands through the taxi window, begging. People defecating and urinating. People clinging to buses. People herding animals. People, people, people, people. As we moved slowly through the mob, hand horn squawking, the dust, noise, heat, and cooking fires gave the scene a hellish aspect. Would we ever get to our hotel? All three of us were, frankly, frightened. It seemed that anything could happen—but, of course, nothing did. Old India hands will laugh at our reaction. We were just some overprivileged tourists, unaccustomed to the sights and sounds of India. Perhaps, but since that night I've known the *feel* of overpopulation.

Too Many People

Americans are beginning to realize that the un-developed countries of the world face an inevita-ble population-food crisis. Each year food produc-tion in undeveloped countries falls a bit further behind burgeoning population growth, and peo-ple go to bed a little bit hungrier. While there are temporary or local reversals of this trend, it now seems inevitable that it will continue to its logi-cal conclusion: mass starvation. The rich are go-ing to get richer, but the more numerous poor are going to get poorer. Of these poor, a minimum of three and one-half million will starve to death this year, mostly children. But this is a mere handful compared to the numbers that will be starving in a decade or so. And it is now too late to take ac-tion to save many of those people.

In a book about population there is a tempta-tion to stun the reader with an avalanche of sta-tistics. I'll spare you most, but not all, of that. Af-ter all, no matter how you slice it, population is a numbers game. Perhaps the best way to im-press you with numbers is to tell you about the "doubling time"—the time necessary for the population to double in size.

It has been estimated that the human population of 6000 B.C. was about five million people, taking perhaps one million years to get there from two and a half million. The population did not reach 500 million until almost 8,000 years later —about 1650 A.D. This means it doubled roughly once every thousand years or so. It reached a billion people around 1850, doubling in some 200 years. It took only 80 years or so for the next doubling, as the population reached two billion around 1930. We have not completed the next doubling to four billion yet, but we now have well over three billion people. The doubling time at present seems to be about 37 years.[1] Quite a reduction in doubling times: 1,000,000 years, 1,000 years, 200 years, 80 years, 37 years. Perhaps the meaning of a doubling time of around 37 years is best brought home by a theoretical exercise. Let's examine what might happen on the absurd assumption that the population continued to double every 37 years into the indefinite future.

If growth continued at that rate for about 900 years, there would be some 60,000,000,000,000,-000 people on the face of the earth. Sixty million billion people. This is about 100 persons for each square yard of the Earth's surface, land and sea. A British physicist, J. H. Fremlin,[2] guessed that such a multitude might be housed in a continuous 2,000-story building covering our entire planet. The upper 1,000 stories would contain only the apparatus for running this gigantic warren. Ducts, pipes, wires, elevator shafts, etc., would occupy about half of the space in the bottom 1,000 stories. This would leave three or four yards of floor space for each person. I will leave to your imagination the physical details of existence in this ant heap, except to point out that all would not be black. Probably each person would be limited in his travel. Perhaps he could take elevators through all 1,000 residential stories but could travel only within a circle of a few hundred yards' radius on any floor. This would permit, however, each person to choose his friends from among some ten million people! And, as Fremlin points out, entertainment on the worldwide TV should be excellent, for at any time "one could expect some ten million Shakespeares and rather more Beatles to be alive."

Could growth of the human population of the Earth continue beyond that point? Not according to Fremlin. We would have reached a "heat limit." People themselves, as well as their activities, convert other forms of energy into heat which must be dissipated. In order to permit this excess heat to radiate directly from the top of the "world building" directly into space, the atmosphere would have been pumped into flasks under the sea well before the limiting population size was reached. The precise limit would depend on the technology of the day. At a population size of one billion billion people, the temperature of the "world roof" would be kept around the melting point of iron to radiate away the human heat generated.

But, you say, surely Science (with a capital "S") will find a way for us to occupy the other planets of our solar system and eventually of other stars before we get all that crowded. Skip for a moment the virtual certainty that those planets are uninhabitable. Forget also the insurmountable logistic problems of moving billions of people off the Earth. Fremlin has made some interesting calculations on how much time we could buy by occupying the planets of the solar system. For instance, at any given time it would take only about 50 years to populate Venus, Mercury, Mars, the moon, and the moons of Jupiter and Saturn to the same population density as Earth.[3]

What if the fantastic problems of reaching and colonizing the other planets of the solar system, such as Jupiter and Uranus, can be solved? It would take only about 200 years to fill them "Earth-full." So we could perhaps gain 250 years of time for population growth in the solar system after we had reached an absolute limit on Earth. What then? We can't ship our surplus to the stars. Professor Garrett Hardin[4] of the University of California at Santa Barbara has dealt effectively with this fantasy. Using extremely optimistic assumptions, he has calculated that Americans, by cutting their standard of living down to 18% of its present level, could in *one year* set aside enough capital to finance the exportation to the stars of *one day's* increase in the population of the world.

Interstellar transport for surplus people presents an amusing prospect. Since the ships would take generations to reach most stars, the only people who could be transported would be those willing to exercise strict birth control. Population explosions on space ships would be disastrous. Thus we would have to export our responsible people, leaving the irresponsible at home on Earth to breed.

Enough of fantasy. Hopefully, you are convinced that the population will have to stop growing sooner or later and that the extremely remote possibility of expanding into outer space offers no escape from the laws of population growth. If you still want to hope for the stars, just remember that, at the current growth rate, in a few thousand years everything in the visible universe would be converted into people, and the ball of people would be expanding with the speed of light![5] Unfortunately, even 900 years is much too far in the future for those of us concerned with the population explosion. As you shall see, the next *nine* years will probably tell the story.

Of course, population growth is not occurring uniformly over the face of the Earth. Indeed, countries are divided rather neatly into two groups: those with rapid growth rates, and those with relatively slow growth rates. The first group, making up about two-thirds of the world population, coincides closely with what are known as the "undeveloped countries" (UDCs). The UDCs are not industrialized, tend to have inefficient agriculture, very small gross national products, high illiteracy rates and related problems. That's what UDCs are technically, but a short definition of undeveloped is "starving." Most Latin American, African, and Asian countries fall into this category. The second group consists, in essence, of the "developed countries" (DCs). DCs are modern, industrial nations, such as the United States, Canada, most European countries, Israel, Russia, Japan, and Australia. Most people in these countries are adequately nourished.

Doubling times in the UDCs range around 20 to 35 years. Examples of these times (from the 1968 figures just released by the Population Reference Bureau) are Kenya, 24 years; Nigeria, 28; Turkey, 24; Indonesia, 31; Philippines, 20; Brazil, 22; Costa Rica, 20; and El Salvador, 19. Think of what it means for the population of a country to double in 25 years. In order just to keep living standards at the present inadequate level, the food available for the people must be doubled. Every structure and road must be duplicated. The amount of power must be doubled. The capacity of the transport system must be doubled. The number of trained doctors, nurses, teachers, and administrators must be doubled. This would be a fantastically difficult job in the United States—a rich country with a fine agricultural system, immense industries, and rich natural resources. Think of what it means to a country with none of these.

Remember also that in virtually all UDCs, people have gotten the word about the better life it is possible to have. They have seen colored pictures in magazines of the miracles of Western technology. They have seen automobiles and airplanes. They have seen American and European movies. Many have seen refrigerators, tractors, and even TV sets. Almost all have heard transistor radios. They *know* that a better life is possible. They have what we like to call "rising expectations." If twice as many people are to be happy, the miracle of doubling what they now have will not be enough. It will only maintain today's standard of living. There will have to be a tripling or better. Needless to say, they are not going to be happy.

Doubling times for the populations of the DCs tend to be in the 50-to-200-year range. Examples of 1968 doubling times are the United States, 63 years; Austria, 175; Denmark, 88; Norway, 88; United Kingdom, 140; Poland, 88; Russia, 63; Italy, 117; Spain, 88; and Japan, 63. These are industrialized countries that have undergone the so-called demographic transition—a transition from high to low growth rate. As industrialization progressed, children became less important to parents as extra hands to work on the farm and as support in old age. At the same time they became a financial drag—expensive to raise and educate. Presumably these are the reasons for a slowing of population growth after industrialization. They boil down to a simple fact—people just want to have fewer children.

This is not to say, however, that population is not a problem for the DCs. First of all, most of them are overpopulated. They are overpopulated by the simple criterion that they are not able to produce enough food to feed their populations. It is true that they have the money to buy food, but when food is no longer available for sale they will find the money rather indigestible. Then, too, they share with the UDCs a serious problem of population distribution. Their urban centers are getting more and more crowded relative to the countryside. This problem is not as severe as it is in the UDCs (if current trends should continue, which they cannot, Calcutta could have 66 million inhabitants in the year 2000). As you are well aware, however, urban concentrations are creating serious problems even in America. In the United States, one of the more rapidly growing DCs, we hear constantly of the headaches caused by growing population: not just garbage in our environment, but overcrowded highways, burgeoning slums, deteriorating school systems, rising crime rates, riots, and other related problems.

From the point of view of a demographer, the whole problem is quite simple. A population will continue to grow as long as the birth rate exceeds the death rate—if immigration and emigration are not occurring. It is, of course, the balance between birth rate and death rate that is critical. The birth rate is the number of births per thousand people per year in the population. The death rate is the number of deaths per thousand people per year.[6] Subtracting the death rate from the birth rate, and ignoring migration, gives the rate of increase. If the birth rate is 30 per thousand per year, and the death rate is 10 per thousand per year, then the rate of increase is 20 per thousand per year (30 — 10 = 20). Expressed as a percent (rate per hundred people), the rate of 20 per thousand becomes 2%. If the rate of increase is 2%, then the doubling time will be 35 years. Note that if you simply added 20 people per thousand per year to the population, it would take 50 years to add a second thousand people (20 × 50 = 1,000). But the doubling time is actually much less because populations grow at compound interest rates. Just as interest dollars themselves earn interest, so people added to populations produce more people. It's growing at compound interest that makes populations double so much more rapidly than seems possible. Look at the relationship between the annual percent increase (interest rate) and the doubling time of the population (time for your money to double):

Annual percent increase	Doubling time
1.0	70
2.0	35
3.0	24
4.0	17

Those are all the calculations—I promise. If you are interested in more details on how demographic figuring is done, you may enjoy reading Thompson and Lewis's excellent book, *Population Problems*.[7]

There are some professional optimists around who like to greet every sign of dropping birth rates with wild pronouncements about the end of the population explosion. They are a little like a person who, after a low temperature of five below zero on December 21, interprets a low of only three below zero on December 22 as a cheery sign of approaching spring. First of all, birth rates, along with all demographic statistics, show short-term fluctuations caused by many factors. For instance, the birth rate depends rather heavily on the number of women at reproductive age. In the United States the current low birth rates soon will be replaced by higher rates as more post World War II "baby boom" children move into their reproductive years. In Japan, 1966, the Year of the Fire Horse, was a year of very low birth rates. There is widespread belief that girls born in the Year of the Fire Horse make poor wives, and Japanese couples try to avoid giving birth in that year because they are afraid of having daughters.

But, I repeat, it is the relationship between birth rate and death rate that is most critical. Indonesia, Laos, and Haiti all had birth rates around 46 per thousand in 1966. Costa Rica's birth rate was 41 per thousand. Good for Costa Rica? Unfortunately, not very. Costa Rica's death rate was less than nine per thousand, while the other countries all had death rates above 20 per thousand. The population of Costa Rica in 1966 was doubling every 17 years, while the doubling times of Indonesia, Laos, and Haiti were all above 30 years. Ah, but, you say, it was good for Costa Rica—fewer people per thousand were dying each year. Fine for a few years perhaps, but what then? Some 50% of the people in Costa Rica are under 15 years old. As they get older, they will need more and more food in a world with less and less. In 1983 they will have twice as many mouths to feed as they had in 1966, if the 1966 trend continues. Where will the food come from? Today the death rate in Costa Rica is low in part because they have a large number of physicians in proportion to their population.

27

How do you suppose those physicians will keep the death rate down when there's not enough food to keep people alive?

One of the most ominous facts of the current situation is that roughly 40% of the population of the undeveloped world is made up of people *under 15 years old.* As that mass of young people moves into its reproductive years during the next decade, we're going to see the greatest baby boom of all time. Those youngsters are the reason for all the ominous predictions for the year 2000. They are the gunpowder for the population explosion.

How did we get into this bind? It all happened a long time ago, and the story involves the process of natural selection, the development of culture, and man's swollen head. The essence of success in evolution is reproduction. Indeed, natural selection is simply defined as differential reproduction of genetic types. That is, if people with blue eyes have more children on the average than those with brown eyes, natural selection is occurring. More genes for blue eyes will be passed on to the next generation than will genes for brown eyes. Should this continue, the population will have progressively larger and larger proportions of blue-eyed people. This differential reproduction of genetic types is the driving force of evolution; it has been driving evolution for billions of years. Whatever types produced more offspring became the common types. Virtually all populations contain very many different genetic types (for reasons that need not concern us), and some are always outreproducing others. As I said, reproduction is the key to winning the evolutionary game. Any structure, physiological process, or pattern of behavior that leads to greater reproductive success will tend to be perpetuated. The entire process by which man developed involves thousands of millenia of our ancestors being more successful breeders than their relatives. Facet number one of our bind—the urge to reproduce has been fixed in us by billions of years of evolution.

Of course through all those years of evolution, our ancestors were fighting a continual battle to keep the birth rate ahead of the death rate. That they were successful is attested to by our very existence, for, if the death rate had overtaken the birth rate for any substantial period of time, the evolutionary line leading to man would have gone extinct. Among our apelike ancestors, a few million years ago, it was still very difficult for a mother to rear her children successfully. Most of the offspring died before they reached reproductive age. The death rate was near the birth rate. Then another factor entered the picture—cultural evolution was added to biological evolution.

Culture can be loosely defined as the body of nongenetic information which people pass from generation to generation. It is the accumulated

29

knowledge that, in the old days, was passed on entirely by word of mouth, painting, and demonstration. Several thousand years ago the written word was added to the means of cultural transmission. Today culture is passed on in these ways, and also through television, computer tapes, motion pictures, records, blueprints, and other media. Culture is all the information man possesses except for that which is stored in the chemical language of his genes.

The large size of the human brain evolved in response to the development of cultural information. A big brain is an advantage when dealing with such information. Big-brained individuals were able to deal more successfully with the culture of their group. They were thus more successful reproductively than their smaller-brained relatives. They passed on their genes for big brains to their numerous offspring. They also added to the accumulating store of cultural information, increasing slightly the premium placed on brain size in the next generation. A self-reinforcing selective trend developed—a trend toward increased brain size.[8]

But there was, quite literally, a rub. Babies had bigger and bigger heads. There were limits to how large a woman's pelvis could conveniently become. To make a long story short, the strategy of evolution was not to make a woman bellshaped and relatively immobile, but to accept the problem of having babies who were helpless for a long period while their brains grew after birth.[9] How could the mother defend and care for her infant during its unusually long period of helplessness? She couldn't, unless Papa hung around. The girls are still working on that problem, but an essential step was to get rid of the short, well-defined breeding season characteristic of most mammals. The year-round sexuality of the human female, the long period of infant dependence on the female, the evolution of the family group, all are at the roots of our present problem. They are essential ingredients in the vast social phenomenon that we call sex. Sex is not simply an act leading to the production of offspring. It is a varied and complex cultural phenomenon penetrating into all aspects of our lives —one involving our self-esteem, our choice of friends, cars, and leaders. It is tightly interwoven with our mythologies and history. Sex in man is necessary for the production of young, but it also evolved to ensure their successful rearing. Facet number two of our bind—our urge to reproduce is hopelessly entwined with most of our other urges.

Of course, in the early days the whole system did not prevent a very high mortality among the young, as well as among the older members of the group. Hunting and food-gathering is a risky business. Cavemen had to throw very impressive cave bears out of their caves before the men could move in. Witch doctors and shamans had a less than perfect record at treating wounds and curing disease. Life was short, if not sweet. Man's total population size doubtless increased slowly but steadily as human populations expanded out of the African cradle of our species.

Then about 8,000 years ago a major change occurred—the agricultural revolution. People began to give up hunting food and settled down to grow it. Suddenly some of the risk was removed from life. The chances of dying of starvation diminished greatly in some human groups. Other threats associated with the nomadic life were also reduced, perhaps balanced by new threats of disease and large-scale warfare associated with the development of cities. But the overall result was a more secure existence than before, and the human population grew more rapidly. Around 1800, when the standard of living in what are today the DCs was dramatically increasing due to industrialization, population growth really began to accelerate. The development of medical science was the straw that broke the camel's back. While lowering death rates in the DCs was due in part to other factors, there is no question that "instant death control," exported by the DCs, has been responsible for the drastic lowering of death rates in the UDCs. Medical science, with its efficient public health programs, has been able to depress the death rate with astonishing rapidity and at the same time drastically increase the birth rate; healthier people have more babies.

The power of exported death control can best be seen by an examination of the classic case of Ceylon's assault on malaria after World War II. Between 1933 and 1942 the death rate due directly to malaria was *reported* as almost two per thousand. This rate, however, represented only a portion of the malaria deaths, as many were reported as being due to "pyrexia."[10] Indeed, in 1934–1935 a malaria epidemic may have been directly responsible for fully half of the deaths on the island. In addition, malaria, which infected a large portion of the population, made people susceptible to many other diseases. It thus contributed to the death rate indirectly as well as directly.

The introduction of DDT in 1946 brought rapid control over the mosquitoes which carry malaria. As a result, the death rate on the island was halved in less than a decade. The death rate in Ceylon in 1945 was 22. It dropped 34% between 1946 and 1947 and moved down to ten in 1954. Since the sharp postwar drop it has continued to decline and now stands at eight. Although part of the drop is doubtless due to the killing of other insects which carry disease and to other public health measures, most of it can be accounted for by the control of malaria.

Victory over malaria, yellow fever, smallpox, cholera, and other infectious diseases has been responsible for similar plunges in death rate throughout most of the UDCs. In the decade

33

1940–1950 the death rate declined 46% in Puerto Rico, 43% in Formosa, and 23% in Jamaica. In a sample of 18 undeveloped areas the average decline in death rate between 1945 and 1950 was 24%.

It is, of course, socially very acceptable to reduce the death rate. Billions of years of evolution have given us all a powerful will to live. Intervening in the birth rate goes against our evolutionary values. During all those centuries of our evolutionary past, the individuals who had the most children passed on their genetic endowment in greater quantities than those who reproduced less. Their genes dominate our heredity today. All our biological urges are for more reproduction, and they are all too often reinforced by our culture. In brief, death control goes with the grain, birth control against it.

In summary, the world's population will continue to grow as long as the birth rate exceeds the death rate; it's as simple as that. When it stops growing or starts to shrink, it will mean that either the birth rate has gone down or the death rate has gone up or a combination of the two. Basically, then, there are only two kinds of solutions to the population problem. One is a "birth rate solution," in which we find ways to lower the birth rate. The other is a "death rate solution," in which ways to raise the death rate— war, famine, pestilence—*find us*. The problem could have been avoided by *population control,* in which mankind consciously adjusted the birth rate so that a "death rate solution" did not have to occur.

Too Little Food

Why did I pick on the next nine years instead of the next 900 for finding a solution to the population crisis? One answer is that the world, especially the undeveloped world, is rapidly running out of food. And famine, of course, could be one way to reach a death rate solution to the population problem. In fact, the battle to feed humanity is already lost, in the sense that we will not be able to prevent large-scale famines in the next decade or so. It is difficult to guess what the exact scale and consequences of the famines will be. But there *will be* famines. Let's look at the situation today.

Everyone agrees that at least half of the people of the world are undernourished (have too little food) or malnourished (have serious imbalances in their diet). The number of deaths attributable to starvation is open to considerable debate. The reason is threefold. First, demographic statistics are often incomplete or unreliable. Second, starving people don't necessarily die of starvation. They often fall victim to some disease as they weaken. When good medical care is available, starvation can be a long, drawn-out process indeed. Third, and perhaps more important, starvation is undramatic. Deaths from starvation go unnoticed, even when they occur as close as Mississippi. Many Americans are under the delusion that an Asian can live happily "on a bowl of rice a day." Such a diet means slow starvation for an Asian, just as it would for an American. A *New Republic* article[11] estimated that five million Indian children die each year of malnutrition. The Population Crisis Committee estimates that three and one-half million people will starve to death this year, mostly children. Senator George McGovern[12] called hunger "the chief killer of man."

Through the first decade following World War II, food production per person in the UDCs kept up with population growth. Then, sometime around 1958, "the stork passed the plow."[13] Serious transfers of food began from the DCs to the UDCs. As food got scarcer, economic laws of supply and demand began to take effect in the UDCs. Food prices began to rise. Marginal land began to be brought into production—as evidenced by reduced yields per acre. In short, all the signs of an approaching food crisis began to appear. Then in 1965–1966 came the first dramatic blow.

In 1965–1966 mankind suffered a shocking

defeat in what is now popularly called the "war on hunger." In 1966, while the population of the world increased by some 70 million people, there was *no* compensatory increase in food production. According to the United Nations Food and Agriculture Organization (FAO), advances in food production made in developing nations between 1955 and 1965 were wiped out by agricultural disasters in 1965 and 1966. In 1966 each person on Earth had 2% less to eat, the reduction, of course, not being uniformly distributed. Only ten countries grew more food than they consumed: the United States, Canada, Australia, Argentina, France, New Zealand, Burma, Thailand, Rumania, and South Africa. The United States produced more than half of the surplus, with Canada and Australia contributing most of the balance. All other countries, including the giants of China, India, and Russia, imported more than they exported. In 1966 the United States shipped *one quarter* of its wheat crop, nine million tons, to India. In the process we helped change the distribution of people in the country. Thousands migrated into port cities so as to be close to the centers of wheat distribution. We also, in the opinion of some, hindered India's own agricultural development. Perhaps we gave too many Indians the impression that we have an unlimited capacity to ship them food. Unhappily, we do not.

In 1967 we were extremely fortunate in having a fine growing year almost worldwide. If the predicted harvests actually materialize (we will not know until some months after this is written), the amount of food produced per person will be 5 or 6% above the 1966 levels. But it will still not be up to the 1964 level. This partial recovery, due largely to good weather, seems to have shifted some agriculturists (especially in the U.S. Department of Agriculture) from pessimism to limited optimism about the world food situation. True, there are hopeful signs, especially in the form of new wheat and rice varieties. But we're not even in a position to evaluate the true potential of these developments, let alone assign to them the panacea role so devoutly wished for by many. More of that later.

Nowhere is hoping more of a habit than in the Indian government. Madan G. Kaul, Minister of the Indian Embassy, addressing the Second International Conference on the War on Hunger, hoped that his country would be self-sufficient in food by 1971. If only hoping would make it so! To put this fantasy into perspective, you must know that this means the Indians hope to be able to feed 50 to 70 million more people in four years than they *cannot* feed today. Their population is growing at a rate of 14 to 18 million people per year.

Let's look at how two experts view the Indian food situation. Dr. Raymond Ewell states:[14]

"In thirteen years India is going to add two

hundred million more people to their population. In my opinion, as an old India hand, I don't see how they can possibly feed two hundred million more people by 1980. They could if they had the time, say until the year 2000. Maybe they could even do it by 1990, but they can't do it by 1980. It's a matter of time, of learning new techniques and doing all the various things that need to be done. They all take time.

"Even the United States would be greatly pressed to provide for two hundred million more people. Say we had two hundred million more people dumped on the United States in thirteen years. We'd have an extremely difficult time feeding them, to say nothing of providing housing and education and transportation, parking spaces for all the cars, etc. It would be an enormous problem for the United States, and yet the United States has a superb industrial plant, very productive agriculture, a good educational system, excellent natural resources, lots of natural gas, petroleum, coal, mineral ores of all types. India has none of these things. And yet India is going to have two hundred million more people in the next thirteen years."

Is Ewell a lone pessimist? Not at all—in fact, I have yet to meet anyone familiar with the situation who thinks India will be self-sufficient in food by 1971, if ever. Louis H. Bean recently told the Second International Conference on the War on Hunger:[15] "My examination of the trend of India's grain production over the past eighteen years leads me to the conclusion that the present 1967–1968 production of about 93 to 95 million tons is at a maximum level. This means that for the next two to three years the chances are two to one that production will range between 88 and 96 million tons, not enough to take care of the needs of the rising population."

India, of course, makes an obvious target. But in other parts of the world the situation is at least as serious. Population is far outstripping food production throughout the "other world." Some of the most depressing situations are found in Latin America. In these largely Catholic countries politicians have generally been far behind those of India in recognizing the root of their problems in overpopulation. As noted earlier, doubling times in many Latin American countries are truly spectacular. And the poverty, hunger, and misery of the people are equally spectacular. The hideous conditions in the urban slums—*favelas* in Brazil, *barriadas* in Peru, *tugurios* in Colombia, *ranchos* in Venezuela—have received wide publicity in the press and popular magazines in recent years. Yet most Americans either do not know or choose to ignore the true depths of the misery and despair in which so many of our southern neighbors spin out their lives. Dry figures unfortunately make little impression. It is hard to grasp the meaning of Peru's doubling time of 23 years. It is easy, however, to grasp the meaning of Peruvian Indian children chewing coca leaves. The leaves are the source of cocaine, which suppresses the children's hunger pains.

Turning to Colombia, we find an almost entirely Catholic country with a doubling time of 22 years. Death control did not reach Colombia until after World War II. Before it arrived, a woman could expect to have two or three children survive to reproductive age if she went through ten pregnancies. Now, in spite of malnutrition, medical technology keeps seven or eight alive. Each child adds to the impossible financial burden of the family and to the despair of the mother. According to Dr. Sumner M. Kalman,[16] the average mother goes through a progression of attempts to limit the size of her family. She starts with ineffective native forms of contraception and moves on to quack abortion, infanticide, frigidity, and all too often to suicide. That's the kind of misery that's concealed behind the dry statistic of a population doubling every 22 years. What do you suppose American families would do if, after the last child was born, the average family had to spend 80% of its income on food? That's the spot the Colombians are in.

Arthur Hopcraft recently has published a book, *Born to Hunger*,[17] which might be described as a "report from the front" of the war on hunger. His record of a 45,000-mile trip through Africa, Asia, and South America has much greater immediacy than any set of population-food production statistics. He visited a Dr. Lema, whose survey of the vicinity of Dar es Salaam, Tanzania, revealed 30% of the children under five to be malnourished. Sixty-five of those children were hospitalized with severe kwashiorkor, a malnutrition disease "in which open sores spread over the flesh, particularly on the thighs and lower body, so that the child looks as if he had been badly burned." Fourteen of these children died. To the west of Dar es Salaam, in a less fertile region, the death rate of children under five is nearly 50%. Hopcraft quotes Dr. Shah of Ajarpura, India, to the effect that the infant mortality rate of 125 per 1,000 births in the area was due to gastro-enteritis, respiratory diseases, and malnutrition. Ajarpura was considered a progressive village, although the majority of the people were malnourished.

From Colombia, Hopcraft reports 100 infant deaths *per day* from malnutrition, supporting the picture of desperation painted by Kalman. From Turkana, Kenya, he reports 6,000 people still living on handouts in famine camps established in 1961. Hopcraft reminds us again of what we must never forget as we contemplate our unprecedented problems—that in all the mess of expanding population, faltering food production, and environmental deterioration are enmeshed miserable, hungry, desperate human beings.

So food production in the UDCs is falling behind population growth. Most of these countries now rely heavily on imports. As the crisis deepens, where will the imports come from? Not from Russia—she herself must import food. Not from Canada, Argentina, or Australia. They need money and will be busy selling to food-short countries, such as Russia, which can afford to buy. From the United States then?

They will get some, perhaps, but not anywhere near enough. Our vast agricultural surpluses are gone. Our agriculture is already highly efficient, so that the prospects of massively increasing our production are dim. And the problems of food transport are vast. No responsible person thinks that the United States can save the world from famine with her food exports, although there is considerable debate as to how long we can put off the day of reckoning.

All of this boils down to a few elementary facts. There is not enough food today. How much there will be tomorrow is open to debate. If the optimists are correct, today's level of misery will be perpetuated for perhaps two decades into the future. If the pessimists are correct, massive famines will occur soon, possibly in the early 1970's, certainly by the early 1980's. So far most of the evidence seems to be on the side of the pessimists, and we should plan on the assumption that they are correct. After all, some two billion people aren't being properly fed in 1968!

A Dying Planet

Our problems would be much simpler if we needed only to consider the balance between food and population. But in the long view the progressive deterioration of our environment may cause more death and misery than any conceivable food-population gap. And it is just this factor, environmental deterioration, that is almost universally ignored by those most concerned with closing the food gap.

It is fair to say that the environment of every organism, human and nonhuman, on the face of the Earth has been influenced by the population explosion of *Homo sapiens*. As direct or indirect results of this explosion, some organisms, such as the passenger pigeon, are now extinct. Many others, such as the larger wild animals of all continents, have been greatly reduced in numbers. Still others, such as sewer rats and house flies, enjoy much enlarged populations. But these are obvious results and probably less important than more subtle changes in the complex web of life and in delicately balanced natural chemical cycles. Ecologists—those biologists who study the relationships of plants and animals with their environments—are especially concerned about these changes. They realize how easily disrupted are ecological systems (called ecosystems), and they are afraid of both the short- and long-range consequences for these ecosystems of many of mankind's activities.

Environmental changes connected with agriculture are often striking. For instance, in the United States we are paying a price for maintaining our high level of food production. Professor LaMonte Cole recently said,[18] ". . . even our own young country is not immune to deterioration. We have lost many thousands of acres to erosion and gullying, and many thousands more to strip mining. It has been estimated that the agricultural value of Iowa farmland, which is about as good land as we have, is declining by 1% per year. In our irrigated lands of the West there is the constant danger of salinization from rising water tables, while, elsewhere, from Long Island to Southern California, we have lowered water tables so greatly that in coastal regions salt water is seeping into the aquifers. Meanwhile, an estimated two thousand irrigation dams in the United States are now useless impoundments of silt, sand, and gravel."

The history of similar deterioration in other parts of the world is clear for those who know how to read it. It stretches back to the cradles of civilization in the Middle East, where in many places deserts now occupy what were once rich and productive farmlands. In this area the process of destruction goes on today, still having, as in the past, ecologically incompetent use of water resources as a major feature. A good example is the building of dams on the Nile, preventing the deposit of nutrient-rich silt that used to accompany annual floods of the river. As almost anyone who remembers his high school geography could have predicted, the result has been a continuing decrease in the productivity of soils in the Nile Delta. As Cole puts it, "The new Aswan high dam is designed to bring another million acres of land under irrigation, and it may well prove to be the ultimate disaster for Egypt." The proposed damming of the Mekong could produce the same results for Vietnam and her neighbors.

Plans for increasing food production invariably involve large-scale efforts at environmental modification. These plans involve the "inputs" so beloved of the agricultural propagandist—especially fertilizers to enrich soils and pesticides to discourage our competitors. Growing more food also may involve the clearing of forests from additional land and the provision of irrigation water. There seems to be little hope that we will suddenly have an upsurge in the level of responsibility or ecological sophistication of persons concerned with increasing agricultural output. I predict that the rate of soil deterioration will accelerate as the food crisis intensifies. Ecology will be ignored more and more as things get tough. It is safe to assume that our use of synthetic pesticides, already massive, will increase. In spite of much publicity, the intimate relationship between pesticides on the one hand and environmental deterioration on the other is not often recognized. This relationship is well worth a close look.

One of the basic facts of population biology—that branch of biology that deals with groups of organisms—is that the simpler an ecosystem is, the more unstable it is. A complex forest, consisting of a great variety of plants and animals, will persist year in and year out with no interference from man. The system contains many elements, and changes in different elements often cancel each other out. Suppose one kind of predator eating mice and rabbits suffers a population decline. For instance, suppose most of the foxes in the forest die of disease? The role of that predator will probably be assumed by another, perhaps weasels or owls. There is no population explosion of mice or rabbits. Such compensation may not be possible in a simpler ecosystem. Similarly, no plant-eating animal (herbivore) feeds on all kinds of plants. So the chance of one kind of herbivore, in a population explosion, completely devouring all the leaves in a mixed woodland is virtually nil.

Man, however, is a simplifier of complex ecosystems and a creator of simple ecosystems. Synthetic pesticides, for instance, are one of man's potent tools for reducing the complexity of ecosystems. Insects which we consider to be pests are most often herbivores: corn earworms, potato beetles, boll weevils, cabbage butterflies, etc. Herbivores ordinarily have larger populations than the meat-eaters (carnivores) which feed on them. There are many more deer than there are mountain lions. Those animals with the largest populations are also those most likely to become genetically resistant to assault with pesticides. The reason is not complicated. The original large populations are just more likely to contain the relatively rare genetic varieties which are already resistant. Individuals of these varieties will survive and breed, and their offspring will be resistant.

There is a second reason why herbivores are more likely to become genetically resistant to pesticides. For millions of years the plants have been fighting them with their own pesticides. Many of the sharp flavors of spices come from chemicals that plants have evolved to poison or repel the insects which are eating them. The insects, in turn, have evolved ways of protecting themselves from the poisons. So the herbivorous insects have been fighting the pesticide war for many millions of years—no wonder they're so good at it.

What happens when a complex ecosystem is treated with a synthetic pesticide? Some of the carnivorous species are exterminated, and the pests become resistant. The ecosystem is simplified by the removal of the carnivores and becomes less stable. Since carnivores can no longer help control the size of the pest population, the pesticide treatments must be escalated to more and more dangerous levels. Ads for insecticides sometimes imply that there is some absolute number of pests—that if we could just eliminate all the "public enemies" things would be dandy. In fact, pesticides often *create* pests. Careless overuse of DDT has promoted to "pest" category many species of mites, little insectlike relatives of spiders. The insects which ate the mites were killed by the DDT, and the mites were resistant to DDT. There you have it—instant pests, and more profits for the agricultural chemical industry in fighting these Frankensteins of their own creation. What's more, some of the more potent miticides the chemists have developed with which to do battle seem to be powerful carcinogens—cancer-producing substances.

When man creates simple ecosystems, he automatically creates ecological problems for himself. For instance, he often plants stands of a single grass—wheat fields and corn fields are familiar examples. These lack the complexity necessary for stability and so are subject to almost instant ruination when not guarded constantly.

51

They are particularly vulnerable because very often the natural anti-insect chemicals have been selected out of the crop plant by plant breeders (these chemicals often don't taste good to us, either!).

Pesticides, of course, also reduce the diversity of life in the soil. Remember, soil is not just crushed rock and decaying organic matter. It contains myriads of tiny plants, animals, and microbes which are essential to its fertility. Damage from pesticides must be added to all of the other sources of soil deterioration active today.

Of all the synthetic organic pesticides, we probably know the most about DDT. It is the oldest and most widely used chlorinated hydrocarbon insecticide. It is not found only where it has been applied. Virtually all populations of animals the world over are contaminated with it. DDT tends to accumulate in fatty tissues. Concentrations in the fat deposits of Americans average 11 parts per million (ppm), and Israelis have been found to have as much as 19.2 ppm. More significant in some ways has been the discovery of DDT residues in such unlikely places as the fat deposits of Eskimos, Antarctic penguins, and Antarctic seals. Seals from the east coast of Scotland have been found with concentrations as high as 23 ppm in their blubber. Pesticide pollution is truly a worldwide problem.

In nature DDT breaks down only very slowly. It will last for decades in soils. A recent study of a Long Island marsh that has been sprayed for 20 years for mosquito control revealed up to 32 pounds per acre of DDT in the upper layer of mud.[19] Unhappily, the way DDT circulates in ecosystems leads to a concentration in carnivores. The danger to life and the reproductive capacity of meat-eating birds may be approaching a critical stage now, and the outlook for man if current trends continue does not seem healthy. The day may come when the obese people of the world must give up diets, since metabolizing their fat deposits will lead to DDT poisoning. But, on the bright side, it is clear that fewer and fewer people in the future will be obese! We must remember that DDT has been in use for only about a quarter of a century. It is difficult to predict the results of another 25 years of application of DDT and similar compounds, especially if those years are to be filled with frantic attempts to feed more and more people.

Concern about the effects of our ecologically incompetent use of synthetic pesticides has been widespread for years, and many environmental biologists have spoken out in futile warning. Perhaps the most famous was Rachel Carson, whose *Silent Spring* became a dramatic best seller. I would also highly recommend Robert L. Rudd's more technical *Pesticides and the Living Landscape*. But those financially involved in the massive production and application of pesticides seem to have only one reaction. They and their hired hands among entomologists heap ridicule and abuse upon the ecologists.

Unfortunately, of course, there are health food extremists and the "no-pesticide-ever-for-any-reason" school which provide ammunition to the pesticide industry, but that doesn't change the facts of the case. It is probably true that the direct and immediate threat to human health in present-day use of synthetic pesticides is not extreme. It is also true that many people have led longer, healthier lives because of pesticides—as in Ceylon. The question of long-term effects on health remains open, however. They are difficult to judge until the long term has passed. Perhaps Dr. Malcolm M. Hargraves, Senior Consultant of the Mayo Clinic, was correct when he states his belief that deaths from use of pesticides in the United States exceeded those caused by automobile accidents. But clearly we are even less likely to give up pesticides and related products for this reason than we are willing to give up automobiles. Pesticide deaths are much less dramatic than head-on collisions.

But present-day practices can be condemned on several other counts. First of all, they are often basically uneconomical, locking the farmer and other users into expensive programs that could be avoided by using ecologically more sophisticated control methods and by reeducating the public. For instance, housewives should be taught to accept certain levels of insect damage in their produce in lieu of the small dose of poison they now get. Secondly, and by far most importantly, there are the simplifying effects on ecosystems discussed above, effects which in many cases may now be irreversible.

One could go on with pesticide horror stories galore. The scientific literature is replete with them. There are stories of dying birds, of mosquito fishes resistant to endrin (a potent insecticide) and excreting so much of the chemical that they kill nonresistant fishes kept in the same aquarium. It is a record of ecological stupidity without parallel. One final specific episode will illustrate how complex and subtle the effects may be. Professor L. B. Slobodkin[20] describes a plan to block the seaward ends of lochs in western Scotland and use them as ponds for raising fishes. One of the problems has been to find ways to raise the young fishes in the laboratory so that they can be "planted" in the ponds. It has been discovered that newly hatched brine shrimp serve as a satisfactory food for the kind of fishes that will be raised. These may be obtained from brine shrimp eggs that are gathered commercially in the United States and sold to tropical fish fanciers for use in feeding young tropical fishes. The American supplies come from two places—the San Francisco Bay Area and the Great Salt Lake Basin in Utah. Sufficient eggs for the project can no longer be obtained from the Bay Area because of the demands of the aquarists, and because large areas of suitable brine shrimp habitat are now subdivisions. Unfortunately, the Utah supply is of no use to the British, since brine shrimp hatched from Utah eggs kill their young fishes. The poisonous quality of the Utah shrimp comes from insecticide residues draining from farmlands in the region. So insecticide pollution in Utah is blocking fish production in Scotland!

Finally, pesticides contribute to the serious problems of general environmental pollution. Professor Cole[21] warned, "It is true that 70% or more of the total oxygen production by photosynthesis occurs in the ocean and is largely produced by planktonic diatoms. It is also true that we are dumping into the oceans vast quantities of pollutants consisting, according to one estimate by the U. S. Food and Drug Administration, of as many as a half-million substances. Many of these are biologically active materials, such as pesticides, radioisotopes, and detergents, to which the Earth's living forms have never before had to try to adapt. No more than a minute fraction of these substances and combinations of them has been tested for toxicity to marine diatoms, or, for that matter, to the equally vital forms of life involved in the cycles of nitrogen and other essential elements. I do not think we are in a position to assert right now that we are not poisoning the marine diatoms and thus bringing disaster upon ourselves."

Since Cole wrote these words, an article in

Science magazine[22] has described reduced photosynthesis in laboratory studies of marine diatoms exposed to DDT. We are, of course, removing many terrestrial areas from oxygen production by paving them. We are also depleting the world's supply of oxygen by burning (oxidizing) vast quantities of fossil fuels and by clearing iron-rich tropical soils in which the iron is then oxidized. When the rate of oxygen consumption exceeds the rate at which it is produced, then the oxygen content of the atmosphere will decrease. As Cole says, "If this [decrease] occurred gradually, its effect would be approximately the same as moving everyone to higher altitudes, a change that might help to alleviate the population crisis by raising death rates." However, photosynthesis by the present plant population of the Earth produces a yearly quantity of oxygen equivalent to only a tiny fraction of the mass of oxygen already accumulated in the atmosphere. If we drastically reduce photosynthesis, oxygen depletion will occur, but probably very slowly. I suspect that other ecological catastrophes accompanying poisoning of the sea and clearing plants from the land would lead to mankind's extinction long before he has to start worrying about running out of oxygen. Food depletion would, of course, be the first and most obvious effect!

If you live in one of our great metropolitan areas, you know very well that pesticides are just one of many factors in the pollution of our planet.

The mixture of filth that is dignified with the label "air" in places like Los Angeles, St. Louis, and New York would not have been tolerated by citizens of those cities 50 years ago. But clean air gradually changed to smog, and nobody paid much attention. Sadly, man's evolution did not provide him with a nervous system that readily detects changes that take place slowly, not in minutes, hours, or days, but over decades. It was important for early man and his nonhuman ancestors to be able to detect rather sudden changes in their environments. The caveman who did not immediately notice the appearance of a cave bear did not survive to pass on his genes for a dull-witted nervous system. Large animals charging, rocks falling, children crying, fires starting— these are the sort of short-range changes that our ancestors had to react to. But the world of 276,824 B.C. was much like that of 276,804 B.C. There was little reason for a creature that only lived an average of perhaps 20 years to learn to deal with environmental changes that occurred over decades. We perceive sudden changes readily, slow changes with difficulty.

If the smog had appeared in Los Angeles overnight, people would have fled gibbering into the hills. But it came on gradually, and man, adaptable organism that he is, learned to live with it. We first paid serious attention to smog when it presented itself as a direct health hazard. Smog disasters years ago in Donora, Pennsylvania, and

58

London, England, produced dead bodies and thus attracted attention. Corpses usually are required to attract the attention of those who pooh-pooh environmental threats—indeed many of my colleagues feel that only a pesticide disaster of large magnitude will produce even a measure of rational control over these substances. The 1952 London incident was blamed for 4,000 deaths, the current record. Since then a clear link between air pollution and respiratory disease has been established. For instance, doctors compared cigarette smokers from smoggy St. Louis with cigarette smokers from relatively smog-free Winnipeg, Canada. There was roughly four times as much emphysema—an unpleasant disease that suffocates its victims—among the group from St. Louis. Pollution also may be linked with certain kinds of heart disease and tuberculosis, not as a cause but as a contributor to higher death rates. In addition to this disease threat there is also the strong suspicion that occurrence of certain cancers is associated with specific pollutants in the air. People now are generally aware of the air pollution problem, at least as far as its direct challenges to health and beauty are concerned. But, once again, the subtle and much more important ecological threats usually remain unrecognized.

One such threat, of course, comes from the killing of plants, many of which have little resistance to smog. Remember, every plant that goes is one less contributor to our food and oxygen supplies. But even more important is the potential for changing the climate of the Earth. All of the junk we dump into the atmosphere, all of the dust, all of the carbon dioxide, have effects on the temperature balance of the Earth. Air pollution affects how much of the sun's heat reaches the surface of the Earth and how much is radiated back into space. And it is just this temperature balance that causes the changes in the atmosphere that we call "the weather."

Concern about this problem has been greatly increased by the prospect of supersonic transports. Most people have been opposing this project on the basis that the "sonic booms" generated will drive half the people in the country out of their skulls while benefiting almost no one. But ecologists, as usual, have been looking at the less obvious. Supersonic transports will leave contrails high in the stratosphere, where they will break up very slowly. A lid of ice crystals gradually will be deposited high in the atmosphere, which might add to the "greenhouse effect" (prevention of the heat of the Earth from radiating back into space). On the other hand, they may produce a greater cooling than heating effect because of the sun's rays which they reflect back into space. One way or another, you can bet their effect will not be "neutral." The greenhouse effect is being enhanced now by the greatly increased level of carbon dioxide in the atmosphere. In the last century our burning of fossil fuels raised the level some 15%. The greenhouse effect today is being countered by low-level clouds generated by contrails, dust, and other contaminants that tend to keep the energy of the sun from warming the Earth in the first place.

At the moment we cannot predict what the overall climatic results will be of our using the atmosphere as a garbage dump. We do know that very small changes in either direction in the average temperature of the Earth could be very serious. With a few degrees of cooling, a new ice age might be upon us, with rapid and drastic effects on the agricultural productivity of the temperate regions. With a few degrees of heating, the polar ice caps would melt, perhaps raising ocean levels 250 feet. Gondola to the Empire State Building, anyone?

In short, when we pollute, we tamper with the energy balance of the Earth. The results in terms of global climate and in terms of local weather could be catastrophic. Do we want to keep it up and find out what will happen? What do we gain by playing "environmental roulette"?

My first job after I got my doctorate was working as a research associate with Dr. Joseph H. Camin, then of the Chicago Academy of Sciences. That was in 1957–1958. Now, ten years later, Joe Camin is spending a sabbatical leave with me at Stanford. The other day Joe and I were reminiscing over some extremely pleasant times we had had working together on a field problem. We had been studying natural selection in water snakes which lived on islands in the western end of Lake Erie. The problem was fascinating, and we would be very much interested in continuing the research today. But all we can do is reminisce. You see, in the past decade Lake Erie has died. The snakes are almost gone, as are the fishes on which they fed. The once beautiful lake is now a septic tank—a stinking mess. In 1955 the lake supported commercial fishing. In that year 75 million pounds of fish were taken. No one in his right mind would eat a Lake Erie fish today, if one could be found.

Lake Erie is just one example of a general problem of pollution of lakes, rivers, and streams in the United States and around the world. Lake Michigan will soon follow it in extinction. A recent *New York Times* article described the reduced chances of Russian conservationists to save Lake Baikal and its unique plant and animal life from a fate similar to that of Lake Erie. Many of the world's rivers are quickly approaching the "too thin to plow and too thick to drink" stage—and carrying to the sea those dangerous compounds discussed above.

Finally, let me mention a pollution problem not limited to air or water. We are constantly adding lead to our environment from ethyl gasoline and pesticides, and it is present also in many common substances such as paints and food-can solder. Some scientists are very much concerned with the quantities of lead found in the bodies of Americans. In some instances these are approaching the levels necessary to produce symptoms of chronic lead poisoning—weakness, apathy, lowered fertility, miscarriage, etc. It is a sobering thought that overexposure to lead was probably a factor in the decline of the Roman Empire. As Dr. S. C. Gilfillian[28] has pointed out, the Romans lined their bronze cooking, eating, and wine storage vessels with lead. They thus avoided the obvious and unpleasant taste and symptoms of copper poisoning. They traded them for the pleasant flavor and more subtle poisoning associated with lead. Lead was also common in Roman life in the form of paints, and lead pipes often were used to carry water. Examination of the bones of upper-class Romans of the classical period shows high concentrations of lead—possibly one cause of the famous decadence of Roman leadership. The lower classes lived more simply, drank less wine from lead-lined containers, and thus may have picked up far less lead. This little horror study should make us all a little more leery of the "corpses before we recognize the problem" school of thought. Chronic low-level effects can be critical, too.

Deterioration of our environment clearly holds threats for our physical well-being, present and future. What about our mental health? Does the deterioration threaten it, too? Are we living in a deteriorating "psychic environment"? Riots, rising crime rates, disaffection of youth, and increased drug usage seems to indicate that we are. Unfortunately, we can't even be sure how much of the reaction of an individual to the deterioration of his environment is hereditarily conditioned, or how much is a product of his culture. At least three biologists, H. H. Iltis, P. Andrews, and O. L. Loucks,[24] feel that nature as well as nurture may be very important, that mankind's genetic endowment has been shaped by evolution to require "natural" surroundings for optimum mental health. These biologists write:

"Unique as we may think we are, we are nevertheless as likely to be genetically programed to a natural habitat of clean air and a varied green landscape as any other mammal. To be relaxed and feel healthy usually means simply allowing our bodies to react in the way for which one hundred millions of years of evolution has equipped us. Physically and genetically, we appear best adapted to a tropical savanna, but as a cultural animal we utilize learned adaptations to cities and towns. For thousands of years we have tried in our houses to imitate not only the climate, but the setting of our evolutionary past: warm, humid air, green plants, and even animal companions. Today, if we can afford it, we may even build a greenhouse or swimming pool next to our living room, buy a place in the country, or at least take our children vacationing on the seashore. The specific physiological reactions to natural beauty and diversity, to the shapes and colors of nature (especially to green), to the motions and sounds of other animals, such as birds, we as yet do not comprehend. But it is evident that nature in our daily life should be thought of as a part of the biological need. It cannot be neglected in the discussions of resource policy for man."

You will note that my discussion of man's environment has not dwelt on the themes that characterize the pleas of conservationists. I haven't discussed the rumor that Governor Reagan will soon announce the construction of a giant vinyl redwood tree that can be trucked around the State of California for all to see (permitting all the other "useless" redwoods to be mowed down by our progressive lumbering industry). I've shed no tears here for the passenger pigeons, now extinct, or the California condors, soon to join them. No tears for them, or for the great auk, or the mammoths, or the great herds of bison, or the California grizzly bears, or the Carolina parakeet. I haven't written about them, or of the pleasantness, beauty, indeed glory of many natural areas. Instead I have concentrated on things that seem to bear most directly on man. The reason is simple. In spite of all the efforts of conservationists, all the propaganda, all the eloquent writing, all the beautiful pictures, the conservation battle is presently being lost. In my years of interest in this question I've come to the conclusion that it is being lost for two powerful reasons. The first, of course, is that nothing "undeveloped" can long stand in the face of the population explosion. The second is that most Americans clearly don't give a damn. They've never heard of the California condor and would shed no tears if it became extinct. Indeed, many Americans would compete for the privilege of shooting the last one. Our population consists of two groups; a comparatively small one dedicated to the preservation of beauty and wildlife, and a vastly larger one dedicated to the destruction of both (or at least apathetic toward it). I am assuming that the first group is with me and that the second cannot be moved to action by an appeal to beauty, or a plea for mercy for what may well be our only living companions in a vast universe.

I have just scratched the surface of the problem of environmental deterioration, but I hope that I have at least convinced you that subtle ecological effects may be much more important than the obvious features of the problem. The causal chain of the deterioration is easily followed to its source. Too many cars, too many factories, too much detergent, too much pesticide, multiplying contrails, inadequate sewage treatment plants, too little water, too much carbon dioxide—all can be traced easily to *too many people.*

CHAPTER 2

THE ENDS OF THE ROAD

Too many people—that is why we are on the verge of the "death rate solution." Let's look briefly at what form that solution might take. The agencies most likely to result in a drastic rise in the death rate in the next few decades are exactly those most actively operating in pre-explosion human populations. They are three of the four apocalyptic horsemen—war, pestilence, and famine. Rapid improvement in public health, advances in agriculture, and improved transport systems have temporarily reduced the efficacy of pestilence and famine as population regulators. Improved technology has, on the other hand, greatly increased the potential of war as a population control device. Indeed, it has given us the means for self-extermination.

It now seems inevitable that death through starvation will be at least one factor in the coming increase in the death rate. In the absence of plague or war, it may be the major factor. It is all too easy, however, for a layman to discount the potential for population control possessed today by plague. It is true that medical science has made tremendous advances against communicable diseases, but that does not mean that these diseases may now be ignored. As population density increases, so does the per capita shortage of medical personnel, so do problems of sanitation, and so do populations of disease-harboring organisms such as rats. In addition, malnutrition makes people weaker and more susceptible to infection. With these changes and with people living cheek by jowl, some of mankind's old enemies, like bubonic plague and cholera, may once again be on the move. As hunger and poverty increase, the resources that nations put into the control of vectors (disease-spreading organisms) may be reduced. Malaria, yellow fever, typhus, and their friends are still around—indeed, malaria is still a major killer and disabler of man. These ancient enemies of *Homo sapiens* are just waiting for the resurgence of mosquitoes, lice, and other vectors, to ride high again.

Viruses present an additional possibility. For reasons that are not entirely understood, virus diseases vary in their seriousness. For instance, viruses may become more potent as they circulate in large populations. It is not inconceivable that we will, one of these days, have a visitation from a "super flu," perhaps much more virulent than the famous killer of 1918–1920. That global epidemic killed some 25 million people. A proportionate mortality in the double 1918 population of the near future would be 50 million people, although modern antibiotics might prevent secondary bacterial infections which presumably killed many in 1918–1920. But what if a much more lethal strain should start going in the starving, more crowded population a few years from now? This could happen naturally or through the escape of a special strain created for biological warfare. Modern transport systems would guarantee its rapid invasion of the far corners of the globe. It would be impossible for vaccines to be produced and distributed in time to affect the course of the epidemic in most areas. A great strain would be placed on facilities for production and distribution of antibiotics. Incapacitation of people in vital transport and agricultural occupations would add to the horror by worsening famine in many areas. A net result of 500 million deaths—one out of every seven people—is not inconceivable. By comparison, during World War II only about one out of 200 human beings died in battle.

Obviously, we cannot discuss all of the possible courses of events as the world crisis deepens. It seems inevitable that world political tensions will increase as the disparity between "haves" and "have-nots" increases and as the penalties of being in a "have-not" nation become more and more severe. Political events will have drastic influences on exactly how the death rate increases. They will affect how much food is grown and how it is distributed. They will affect the possibilities of plague. They will affect birth rates, especially in DCs. They will affect the chances of effective international action. The possibilities are infinite; the single course of events that will be realized is unguessable. We can, however, look at a few possibilities as an aid to our thinking, using a device known as a "Scenario." Scenarios are hypothetical sequences of events used as an aid in thinking about the future, especially in identifying possible decision points. I'd like to offer three brief scenarios, giving three possible projections of what the next fifteen years or so could be like. Remember, these are just possibilities, not predictions. We can be sure that none of them will come true as stated, but they describe the kinds of disasters that *will* occur as mankind slips into the famine decades.

SCENARIO I. In 1972 news of the war in Thailand occupies the headlines in the United States. China has had catastrophic floods, a breakdown of communications, and massive famines. Increasingly serious food riots in China, India, and Brazil are a matter of great concern to the Central Intelligence Agency. Ominously, Chinese propaganda blames U.S. political intervention for Canada's refusal to sell further wheat to China. Chinese "volunteer" troops along the 1970 Vietnam truce line are involved in a growing number of truce violation incidents. The

United States mounts a counter propaganda campaign. She claims that China is attempting to distract her starving population with foreign adventures. Russia is disturbed by mounting Chinese border pressure. The U.S.S.R. is increasingly dependent on Canada's dwindling wheat reserves. In early January, 1973, large numbers of Chinese troops move into the Thai conflict for the first time. They receive tactical air support from bases in North Vietnam. The United States is afraid of losing the war in Thailand in spite of her massive troop commitments. The President orders strikes at North Vietnamese air bases with carrier and land-based aircraft. China claims that these air strikes violate the 1970 Geneva truce. She steps up her propaganda line that North American gangsters are getting fat while their puppets control the Mekong rice bowl and permit Asians to starve. Late in January, under cover of monsoon weather, Chinese troops attack southward across the truce line. The United States is faced with a two-front war in Southeast Asia. Food and water rationing are extended. On the home front there is rising anger at the prospect of further sacrifices "to save Asians who clearly don't want to be saved." The U.S. government decides that the time has come at last to apply the full weight of its military might. After an unheeded warning, tactical nuclear weapons are used in strikes on selected Chinese air bases, supply complexes, and staging areas in North

Vietnam, Thailand, and southern China. With the connivance of the Russians a preemptive strike is also launched against China's nuclear facilities. Unfortunately, our defenses are not sufficient to prevent five "dirty" Chinese thermonuclear devices, transported in submarines, from being detonated in the sea off our West Coast. Fallout results in more than 100 million American deaths.

A bad scene, you may say, but it is not the worst possible by any means. Let's look at another possible sequence of events:

SCENARIO II. In 1979 the last non-Communist government in Latin America, that of Mexico, is replaced by a Chinese-supported military junta. The change occurs at the end of a decade of frustration and failure for the United States. Famine has swept repeatedly across Asia, Africa, and South America. Food riots have often become anti-American riots, as our enemies claimed we were withholding food from the starving. In Southeast Asia the Vietnam, Thai, and Laotian wars have resulted in massive casualties, economic crises, and eventual withdrawal to the MacDougal line. Behind that line Australian, Malaysian, and American troops face the growing power of Red China and her allies. As the massive famines swept across Latin America, a series of armed interventions by the United States had proved inadequate to stem the revolutionary tide. During the Mediterranean crisis of 1978 the joint Mexican-United States expeditionary force had been withdrawn from Costa Rica, and the last American "volunteers" withdrawn from Chile. Only the outbreak of a particularly virulent strain of bubonic plague killing 65% of the starving Egyptian population had averted a direct Soviet-American clash in the Mediterranean.

In 1977 both superpowers had withdrawn all aid and influence from the Indian subcontinent as India fell apart into a large number of starving, warring minor states. In her entire history the United States has never faced such a generally hostile world as she does in 1979. Western European nations, living in ever-greater austerity, side with the Soviet Union, accusing the United States of waging biological warfare against the Egyptians. They are joined in their denunciation by Pope Pius XIII who also accuses the United States of "eating meat while the hungry of the world lack bread." In the United States there is actually less meat to eat than at any stage in our history, and price and wage controls and dollar devaluation are an old story. Food and water rationing are standard. Many cities are cycling regularly between riots and uneasy peace under martial law. Nearly complete polarization of opinion exists between the far left groups advocating a complete withdrawal from the international scene and the far right advocating more military action. The government, now virtually a left-right coalition, is under extreme pressure from both sides. It finds any effective action difficult to take.

The Mexican Coup hits President Montgomery at a time of profound internal crisis. The third Los Angeles killer smog in two years has wiped out 90,000 people. Troops holding the city under martial law are under constant attack by rioters. The President's Environmental Advisory Board has reported a measurable rise in the sea level due to melting of the polar ice caps. The Board states further that the decline in fisheries in both the Atlantic and Pacific is now irreversible due to pollution and recommends the immediate compulsory restriction of births to one per couple, and compulsory sterilization of all persons with I.Q. scores under 90. It says that, unless the population size in the United States is reduced rapidly, it too will be facing massive famine by the year 2000. The Emergency Agricultural Commission Report indicates that additional desperate efforts to increase agricultural output would only further reduce production. It recommends a moratorium on the now "overkill" synthetic pesticides. This is required if there is to be any chance of restoring reasonable soil fertility in devastated areas of California and the Middle West, and if biological controls are to be used against the new resistant pests. Pollution and pesticide poisonings have supplanted cardiovascular disease as the number one killer of Americans.

In early 1980 the Chinese and Russians jointly begin to establish missile bases and other military facilities throughout Latin America. They announce a new policy of containing American aggression. In the United States right-wing pressure to launch preemptive nuclear strikes against both China and Russia becomes extreme. Sino-Russian intelligence, estimating that the President will yield to pressure, recommends a first strike by Communist forces. This advice is acted upon, and a general thermonuclear war ensues. Particularly devastating are the high altitude "flash" devices designed to set fire to all flammable materials over huge areas. At one point 15 monster fires rage in the Northern Hemisphere. Each covers an average area of 400,000 square miles—four times the area of Colorado. Inside and outside of these areas, wherever conditions permit, huge fire storms are generated. The effects include rising radiation levels and climatic catastrophe resulting from the addition of enormous amounts of debris and carbon dioxide to the atmosphere. These and general sterilization of the soil (followed by massive erosion) make the northern two-thirds of the Earth uninhabitable. Pollution of the sea is vastly increased. Small pockets of *Homo sapiens* hold on for a while in the Southern Hemisphere, but slowly die out as social systems break down, radiation poisoning takes effect, climatic changes kill crops, livestock dies off, and various man-

77

made plagues spread. The most intelligent creatures ultimately surviving this period are cockroaches.

Now let's see if we can construct a cheerful scenario for number three:

SCENARIO III. In 1974 the United States government finally realizes that the food-population balance in much of Asia, Africa, and South America is such that most areas cannot attain self-sufficiency. American expeditionary forces are withdrawn from Vietnam and Thailand, and the United States announces it will no longer send food to India, Egypt, and some other countries which it considers beyond hope. A moderate food rationing program is instituted in the United States. It further announces that food production in the United States will be increased only so long as the increase can be accomplished without damage to the environment of the North American continent. Pope Pius XIII, yielding to pressure from enlightened Catholics, announces that all good Catholics have a responsibility to drastically restrict their reproductive activities. He gives his blessing to abortion and all methods of contraception. Several cheap, long-term anticonception drugs are developed and made available for wide distribution. Famine and food riots sweep Asia. In China, India, and other areas of Asia, central governments weaken and then disappear. Japan and Australia become the dominant Asian powers, forming a tight, pro-American alliance which is the natural end-point of an economic situation developing since the early 1960's. Russia has serious internal problems, stemming in no small part from her faltering food production and massive aid commitments. Famine and plague sweep the Arab world, which, in the face of Russia's growing disinterest, is forced to seek peace and cooperation with Israel. Israel, in grave economic trouble, installs a peace government and begins negotiations. Most of the countries of Africa and South America slide backward into famine and local warfare. Many adopt Communistic governments, but few are able to achieve any stability. Most of the governments soon control little or no territory, and none represents a threat to the developed sections of the world. In the United Nations, the United States, Canada, Russia, Japan, Australia, and the Common Market countries set up a machinery for "area rehabilitation" which will involve simultaneous population control, agricultural development, and limited industrialization, to be carried out jointly in selected sections of Asia, Africa, and South America. The plan is to be initiated in 1985, when it is calculated that the major die-back will be over, using famine relief distribution stations as bases for both facilities and personnel. The plan will eventually cover the entire world and is programed with a goal of a total world population of two billion in 2025, and 1.5 billion in 2100.

This scenario has considerably more appeal than the others, even though it presumes the death by starvation of perhaps as many as half a billion people, one-fifth of the world's population. Unfortunately, it also involves a maturity of outlook and behavior in the United States that seems unlikely to develop in the near future. I will leave you to decide which scenario is more realistic, and I challenge you to create one more optimistic than the last. (I won't accept one that starts, "In early 1972 the first monster space ships from a planet of the star Alpha Centauri arrive bearing CARE packages . . .")

CHAPTER 3

WHAT IS BEING DONE

Family Planning and Other Failures

A ship has hit the rocks and is sinking. The passengers scream for help. Some jump overboard and are devoured by the circling sharks. A group of distinguished scientists is on board. One of their number suggests that they can help man the pumps. "Oh, no!" shout the others. "That might hurt the captain's feelings. Besides, pumping is not our business. It's outside our field of competence." You can guess what they do. They appoint a committee to study the problem, with subcommittees on marine engineering and navigation. They announce to the passengers that in two or three years the committee will produce a wonderful report which will be acceptable to the passengers, the captain, and the steamship line. Not so passive are the politicians. Some jump up to say that the passengers don't understand the political realities of the situation. Other more progressive politicians grab thimbles and start bailing, stopping every few seconds to accept praise for their valiant efforts.

That about sums up the situation on the population control front in the United States and in much of the rest of the world. People in positions of power have either ignored the problem or have recommended solutions that are inadequate in scope or proven failures. The Catholic Church recommends the rhythm method of contraception. Unfortunately, people who practice this method of contraception are commonly called "parents." Even under the most carefully controlled conditions women using this technique run a 15% risk of pregnancy each year they use it. (With the Pill comparable rates are less than 1%.) Of course, under normal conditions, the failure rate is much higher, about 25%. In short, the rhythm method doesn't work—the irreverent description of it as "Vatican roulette" is, alas, accurate. As Vatican roulette is to family planning, so family planning is to population control. Family planning doesn't work either.

The failure of family planning in the field of population control has been brilliantly outlined by Kingsley Davis in a recent article in the magazine *Science*.[25] He points out that, "The things that make family planning acceptable are the very things that make it ineffective for population control. By stressing the right of parents to have the number of children they want, it evades the basic question of population policy, which is how to give societies the number of children they need. By offering only the means of *couples* to control fertility, it neglects the means for societies to do so." Or, as Justin Blackwelder once said, " 'Family planning' means, among other things, that if we are going to multiply like rabbits, we should do it on purpose. One couple may plan to have three children; another couple may plan seven. In both cases they are a cause of the population problem—not a solution to it." Above all, remember that planned, well-spaced children will starve, or vaporize in a thermonuclear war, or die of plague just as well as unplanned children.

The story in the UDCs is depressingly the same everywhere—people *want* large families. They *want* families of a size that will keep the population growing. "Family planning" is all too often used to lock the barn door after the horse is stolen. Davis reports that among 5,196 women seeking assistance in rural Punjab, India, two-thirds were over 30. Since many were married before they were 15, it is hardly surprising that more than half of them already had six or more children. Similarly, the president of the Hong Kong Family Planning Association pointed out that, at least in the early years of their program, "The patients who received assistance were usually about thirty-one years of age and had six children." It is important to remember that, even if women in the UDCs had exactly the number of children they wanted, the results would still be demographic catastrophe. Family planning is important from the point of view of the health and welfare of individuals, but it does not control populations.

Current birth control programs in the UDCs have their base in "family planning." Their goals are expressed, in almost all cases, in lowered birth rates. Pakistan aims to reduce its birth rate from 50 to 40 per thousand by 1970. India aims to reduce its birth rate from 40 to 25 "as soon as possible." But remember, the critical thing is the *balance* between birth and death rates. With death rates around 10 to 20, it is clear that even achieving these goals could not, by any stretch of the imagination, be called "population control." People would still be multiplying like rabbits and populations doubling every 30 to 40 years.

Let's take a look at family planning in India —a country whose government has been more than a decade ahead of ours in *recognizing* that population size is a matter for governmental concern and action. The Indian government has had an official birth control program since 1951. In the early years of their program they did a lot of experimenting with the rhythm method—although millions of Catholic couples could have given them the word on its efficiency. But recently they've gotten down to business. When I was in Delhi in 1966, posters that said, "Use loop for family planning," were much in evidence. The "loop," of course, refers to several different kinds of plastic devices which, inserted in the womb, prevent conception. These intrauterine devices (IUDs) are one of the main tools of family planning in India. Others are the simple and harmless male sterilization operation, the vasectomy, and the distribution of rubber sheaths (condoms).

In early 1968 Joseph Lelyveld[26] reported that only a small number of India's 335 districts had on hand a complete task force for birth control. One of these few districts is Kaira, an area in which each village has assigned to it a family planning worker. But after having active family planning workers in the district for eight years, its birth rate is higher than the national average. Lelyveld told of the high hopes with which the IUD was greeted as a panacea for India's family planning problems—it was cheap, easily administered, and relatively permanent. But the high hopes were not realized. Although there was an initial spurt of enthusiasm, soon the number of insertions dropped to virtually zero. A principal reason was a series of rumors, some of which were alleged to have been spread by the Bombay office of an American drug company interested in pushing the Pill. The loop was supposed to stick copulating couples together. It was supposed to swim through the bloodstream to the brain. It was supposed to cause excess menstrual bleeding. It was supposed to cause cancer. It was supposed to give the man a shock during intercourse. Small wonder women shied away!

Efforts have been made to squelch the rumors, with some success. Unfortunately, the IUDs do cause increased menstrual bleeding in a small proportion of the women, which made anti-rumor activities more difficult. In some areas the loop is again playing a role, but in the Kaira district it is not.

More recently I have heard the disturbing rumor that in some areas of India women are removing the IUDs so that they can collect again the small payment for having it inserted. Clearly, India has a long way to go with the IUDs.

What about vasectomies? Recently there was talk in India of compulsory sterilization for all males who were fathers of three or more children. Ignore for a moment the socio-political problems that would be raised by such a program. Consider just the logistic problems, as A. S. Parkes did recently.[27] Even if those eligible could be rounded up, it would take 1,000 surgeons or para-surgeons operating eight hours a day, five days a week, a full eight years to sterilize the candidates who exist today. And the stock of candidates is growing very rapidly. Can you picture the probable results of a government attempt to sterilize 40 million American males? What a problem it would be in our country, with its relatively informed populace and efficient transport and communications system! Imagine such an attempt in India, where the difference between castration and sterilization (still not clear to many Westerners) would be almost impossible to explain. As one might expect, the principal Indian official thinking in such tough-minded terms, Dr. S. Chandrasekhar, has recently ended up in a less influential position in a government shuffle.

At the time of this writing (April 1968), the most recent word I have seen on family planning in India is from a Washington *Post* story of March 7, 1968, by Bernard Nossiter. He gives another very depressing report of the failure thus far of the birth control campaign in rural India. The following sample statements will give the flavor of the article:

". . . a Hindu father of three blurts out, 'It is a sin to prevent children from being born.' "

"A grizzled farmer breaks in angrily and says, 'You must practice self-control.' "

"[This] crew is responsible for fifty-nine thousand persons in more than one hundred villages. In the ten months of active campaigning only forty-seven vasectomies have been performed, twenty-seven loops inserted, and very few free condoms accepted."

What then, in summary, is the record of family planning in India? At the start of the program the Indian population growth rate was around 1.3% per year, and the population was some 370 million. After 16 years of effort at family planning, the growth rate was pushing 3% per year, and the population was well over 500 million.

In fact, I know of no country in the world that has achieved true population control through family planning programs (or in any other way). The often quoted examples of Taiwan and Korea are countries undergoing demographic transition where the role of family planning programs was at the most very small. Furthermore, their growth rates have been slowed, not brought to zero. Japan lowered its growth rate dramatically, but not through conventional family planning. A modern, industrialized nation with highly efficient agriculture, Japan was faced, after World War II, with a series of cramped islands and with no opportunity to expand. Both government and industry in Japan supported the program of population control. Its dramatic halving of the birth rate was achieved originally through the sanctioning of abortion. Abortion is a highly effective weapon in the armory of population control. It is condemned by many family planning groups—which are notorious for pussyfooting about methodology, despite their beginning 60 years ago as revolutionary social pioneers. The United Nations, for instance, does not include abortion in family planning. Quite the contrary, the U.N. justifies family planning as a method of combating abortion! Recently Japan's industry, feeling the competition from other Asian countries with cheap labor pools, has withdrawn its support from the population control picture. Japan's growth rate is now rising again. At any rate, the situations in Taiwan, Korea, and Japan are in no way equivalent to those in most UDCs. We would be foolish in the extreme to count on similar sequences of events taking place in other parts of Asia, in Africa, or in Latin America.

What is the government of the United States doing in the area of population control? It is bailing the sinking ship with a very small and leaky thimble. Six federal agencies are involved in one way or another with family planning: Department of Health, Education, and Welfare (HEW); Office of Economic Opportunity (OEO); National Science Foundation (NSF); Department of the Interior; Department of State; and the Agency for International Development (AID). The total spent by the agencies in 1967 for birth control and/or family planning activities was $33 million: $18 million by HEW, $9 million by AID, $5 million by OEO, and $1 million by the others. In 1968 the expenditure of $56 million is programed. These expenditures may seem impressive, but they can be put into perspective easily. For 1968 the entire proposed budget of HEW is about $13.2 billion, and the birth control/planning part is less than one-quarter of one percent! Again, the population budget of all the agencies would not buy more than a dozen sophisticated military jets. It is roughly the same amount as the government appropriation for rat control.

So it's less than a drop in the bucket, not even a good micro-drop, since so much of it is frittered away in family planning. Little is done on population control on a world scale. Here is what

89

Senator Gruening from Alaska had to say before the Senate on May 3, 1967:

"At my request . . . executive agency spokesmen reported to the Government Operations Subcommittee on Foreign Aid Expenditures concerning their activities and efforts to implement President Johnson's mandates. Their reports were disappointing and in no respect implemented President Johnson's mandate for 'new ways to use our knowledge to help deal with the explosion in world population and the growing scarcity in world resources.' They revealed that progress in implementing any programs was painfully slow and that existing programs were inadequately funded and staffed. For example, the subcommittee found that while eleven hundred persons in the Agency for International Development worked on food problems, no more than eleven worked on population problems. Nevertheless, there has been some slight progress."

Senator Gruening has been a leader among the small group of dedicated people in Congress who have been trying to get the government moving on these matters. If we manage to get through the coming crisis, the American people—indeed, the people of the world—will owe a great debt to these men. Their fight is uphill every inch of the way, and progress with the entrenched bureaucrats has been slow indeed. Unfortunately, many of our other legislators are still much more concerned with death control than population control.

Recently there has been a considerable flap involving the Senate and the medical profession over the legal problems involved in transplantation of human organs. Yet this problem is completely insignificant compared with those we have been considering. Unless action is taken on the population front soon, human organ transplants will become an historical curiosity—if history continues. Some way must be found to convince the American people and their elected representatives that continued preoccupation with the problems and diseases of middle age may well prevent today's youngsters from reaching that age. Over the past 20 years an extremely effective lobby in Washington has promoted death control. This group, called by Elizabeth Brenner Drew[28] "The Health Syndicate," has been instrumental in developing and maintaining an extremely high level of federal support of biomedical research—especially on cancer and diseases of the circulatory system. The syndicate, consisting of wealthy and powerful laymen aligned with a selected group of physicians and influential Congressmen, has been strongly criticized for its preoccupation with certain diseases. There has, however, been little effective criticism of the syndicate or the government for their preoccupation with death control. That reduction of the death rate in a population will lead to disaster if the birth rate remains uncontrolled is not recognized. (One of the most important roles of sex education must be to impress on everyone that death control in the absence of birth control is self-defeating, to say the least.)

One might think that American scientists, especially biologists, would be using their influence to get the government moving. Unfortunately they are all too often a retrograde influence. The establishment in American biology consists primarily of death-controllers: those interested in intervening in population processes only by lowering death rates. They have neither the background nor the inclination to understand the problem. The situation is typified by the behavior of the Committee on Population of the National Academy of Sciences—the prototype of the group on the sinking ship busily studying marine engineering. Their big contribution to the whole problem so far (aside from two reports) has been a pompous commentary in *Science* magazine[29] on the accurate and well-documented article by Professor Davis, which I quoted above. Their statement would make instructive reading for anyone concerned with the reasons for the lack of effective population control measures in the world today. The Committee informs us that a zero rate of population growth "may be essential in the long run, but as a goal within the time horizon of current policy it has little support in either the developing or the developed worlds, certainly not among governments." I suppose if the world's governments decree it, the laws of nature will just have to step aside and let mankind turn the universe into solid people!

Anyone not familiar with the death grip the cancer researchers and transplant mechanics have on the political power in biology might be amazed to learn that the Population Committee does not include even one competent ecologist. It does, however, contain several people who have been strongly involved in the family planning movement. Do you suppose that's why they're peddling such totally unsupported statements as, "Family planning may well create its own dynamic in fostering further acceptance"? It is too bad that the Committee, instead of reminding us about unhappy political realities, isn't using its position of prominence to try to change those realities. (Since this was written, I have had the opportunity of discussing the problem with Professor W. D. McElroy, Chairman of the Committee. He agrees almost completely with Davis's view and feels that the Committee did not represent itself accurately in its letter. My personal experiences indicating that committees are poor devices for getting action have thus been further reinforced. I was delighted to learn that Professor McElroy, a distinguished and influential scientist, is taking personal action to help get things moving in our Establishment. I hope that many other scientists will follow his example.)

In summary, the world population control situation is dismal. The principal dim sources of "hope" are the attitudes and actions of governments like those of India, Pakistan, Chile, and other UDCs. They at least realize there is a problem and are trying to take action. Another small hope has been Sweden's activity in pioneering birth control assistance to UDCs. Our own disgraceful puttering really cannot be dignified even by the term "efforts." It is ironic that some Latin American politicians have accused the United States of attempting to pressure them into population control programs. If only it were true!

Multiplying Bread

In a famous 1965 speech before the United Nations, Pope Paul VI stated, "You must strive to multiply bread so that it suffices for the tables of mankind, and not, rather, favor an artificial control of birth, which would be irrational, in order to diminish the number of guests at the banquet of life." We have already seen that the "banquet of life" is, for at least one half of humanity, a breadline or worse. Let's take a look at what is being done at the moment to "multiply bread."

Is there a hope of making today's miserable existence for that half of humanity into a true banquet? Many people seem to feel that the bread can be multiplied. An editorial writer for the *Saturday Evening Post*[30] recently cited "hopeful experts" to the effect that much of the Earth's surface is uncultivated and that the sea contains "unmeasurable riches." He concluded that, with our technological resources, we could perhaps feed the rest of the world indefinitely. This is an absurd extreme of technological optimism, but it is representative of the attitudes of a large number of uninformed Americans, "experts" and non-experts alike.

Can we expect great increases in food production to occur through the placing of more land under cultivation? The answer is a most definite *no*. In almost all instances land that is not farmed today is not farmed for excellent reasons—bad soil, lack of water, unsuitable climate, or some combination of these. In many cases attempts have been made to farm the land and they have failed. When I talk about the population crisis to groups of businessmen, one theme reappears consistently during the question period. It is usually phrased something like this: "I just took a jet to Chicago and noticed that there is a lot of empty country in Nevada. Can't we just farm that country and greatly increase our food production?" The answer is yes and no. Yes, we could farm some of that country—we could farm the surface of the moon if we put enough money, energy, and effort into it. No, we won't do it, at least not in time to affect the coming crisis. The expense would make it economically impossible. I usually point out that supplying water to Nevada's deserts would be one of the most serious problems, though not the only one. Inevitably someone in the audience disagrees—after all, commercial desalting of the oceans is becoming a reality.

So it is. But commercial desalting, at least in

the next few decades, is going to be one of those "thimble-bailing" operations. If the rosiest predictions of the commercial interests working on desalting come true, we will have a worldwide desalting capacity of 20 billion gallons a day in 1984. Pretty impressive, until you learn that the United States alone will need 600 billion gallons of water a day in 1984—two-thirds more than the 360 billion gallons used today. That is, the maximum *world* desalting capacity will be able to supply 1/30th of the needs of *our country* in 1984. And, of course, there is always that little problem of getting the water from the seaside desalting plant 300 to 500 miles inland and almost a mile uphill. Farmers of the Nevada desert had better be prepared to pay a pretty price for the precious fluid, especially since they will be competing with home users and industry. The competition will be rugged, for if our current rape of the watersheds, our population growth, and our water use trends continue, in 1984 the United States will quite literally be dying of thirst.

Unfortunately all flat land isn't farmable. The Russians have recently given us a graphic example of the stupidity of attempting to put marginal land into production. In 1954 large sections of the dry plains of Kazakhstan were put into grain production. Khrushchev had hopes for this highly touted "virgin" lands program, but unfortunately the virgin was a harlot in disguise. Bad climate and other factors turned the program into a major disaster.

It is in the tropics, however, that being seduced by virgin lands is most dangerous. How often must we listen to the ignorant telling us that the population of Brazil can be fed simply by clearing and farming the Amazon Basin? Even disregarding the possible effects of such a project on our future supply of oxygen, the results of trying to farm the basin would be an unmitigated disaster. *Soils in most of the tropical areas of the world are extremely poor.* The lush forests that fill the Amazon Basin today are covering a soil which, if exposed to the sun and air, will quickly become infertile or, as a result of complex chemical changes, even turn to a rocklike substance known as laterite. This has already happened over wide areas of the tropics. Those of us who have been fortunate enough to visit Ankor Wat in Cambodia have seen magnificent cities and temples built by the Khmer civilizations some 800 years ago. The construction materials were sandstone and *laterite*. Unfortunately for the Khmers, as they farmed the local land, it turned to laterite, great for building durable temples, impossible for growing food. The material that gave their civilization its enduring monument also was probably the major cause of its death!

Farming small clearings for a year or two and then letting the jungle reclaim them is the ancient method of agriculture in many areas with soils subject to laterization. At the moment it still seems to be the best way, at least until we develop an agricultural technology for dealing with lateritic soils. Laterization is continuing throughout the tropics and will doubtless proceed more rapidly as mankind gets increasingly desperate for food. Dr. Mary McNeil[31] states, "The ambitious plans to increase food production in the tropics to meet the pressure of the rapid rise of population have given too little consideration to the laterization problem and the measures that will have to be undertaken to overcome it." She goes on to describe the debacle at Iata in the Amazon Basin, where the government of Brazil attempted to found a farming community. Laterization destroyed the project as "in less than five years the cleared fields became virtually pavements of rock."

Let's turn to the other panacea mentioned by our man at the *Saturday Evening Post.* What about those "unmeasurable riches" in the sea? Unhappily, they have been measured and found wanting. The notion that we can extract vastly greater amounts of food from the sea in the near future is quite simply just another myth promoted by the ignorant or the irresponsible. Wherever I go, people ask me about our "farming" of the sea and are invariably shocked by my answer. We are not "farming" the sea today, and to my knowledge there is not a single group in the United

States even attempting to find out how to go about it. In general, man hunts the sea, and occasionally he herds its animals. About the only planting and harvesting of marine crops that man does is some seaweed culture in Japan, and this is really best viewed as an extension of agriculture techniques into the sea. "Farming" the open sea will present an entirely different array of problems.

If we are ever greatly to increase our food yield from the sea, we must learn how to breed and harvest the minute plants (phytoplankton) that are the saltwater equivalents of the plants that our ancestors developed by breeding programs: wheat, corn, rice, and so forth. Then we must find a way to convert the harvest into something people will eat. Getting a high yield from the ocean means going to the primary production— to the plants. Also on land, if we want the most food produced per acre, we must eat the plants. The reason is quite simple. If you have had elementary physics, you will realize that it is the Second Law of Thermodynamics. The law says, in part, that when energy is transferred, some of it becomes unusable at each transfer. Each time energy is transferred in an ecosystem, some of it is converted into heat energy which is not usable by the organisms in the system.

Consider a simple example of what ecologists call a "food chain." A plant is eaten by an insect which is eaten by a trout which in turn is eaten by you. The plant has bound some of the energy of the sun in the chemical bonds of its molecules. The insect extracts that energy and uses some of it to make insect tissues. The trout, in turn, extracts some of the energy in the insect and uses some of it to make trout. Finally you extract some of the energy in the trout and make it into *Homo sapiens*. In transfers of this type only 10 to 20% of the energy present in what was eaten at stage one turns up as usable energy at stage two. To put it another way (using the lower efficiency figure), 1,000 calories of plant make 100 calories of insect which makes ten calories of trout which makes one calorie of person. By skipping the insect and trout links in the food chain, we could get 1,000 calories input simply by eating the plant ourselves, rather than settling for ten calories of trout. Similarly, 100 calories of grain suitable for human consumption but fed to cattle produce at most 10 to 20 calories worth of meat. For this reason, as the world gets hungrier, we will feed lower and lower on the food chains, meat will get more and more expensive, and most of us will become vegetarians. That is also why the only hope for increasing our yield from the sea many-fold lies in farming and eating its plants —something we are not doing and have not the slightest idea how to do.

It is true that we might increase our hunting-herding yield from the sea; indeed, if we were very clever and lucky, we might manage a sustained yield of something like double that of to-day—perhaps even more. To do so would involve research and a great deal of international co-operation to avoid polluting the sea and decreasing our take from overfishing. It would also take some changes in dietary habits, since part of the increase would have to be produced in the form of fish protein concentrate and similar somewhat-less-than-succulent delicacies. Can we expect international cooperation to increase rapidly enough to make a real dent in the problem over the next critical decade or two? I doubt it.

I suspect that international attempts to deal cooperatively with dwindling food resources will at best lead to situations such as those existing to-day in certain fisheries and in the international whaling industry. For years there has been an International Whaling Commission attempting to prevent the overfishing of whales. Their attempts have been a total failure. The industry has not regulated the size and composition of its catch, and as a result the most economically important whale species have been virtually exterminated. Before 1940 there were an estimated 140,000 blue whales in the oceans around Antarctica. In 1954 the total population of these whales was between 10,000 and 14,000. In 1963 the total number was down to somewhere between 650 and 2,000. Capture of blue whales has now been outlawed by the Commission, but their population size may already have been pushed below the point where it could recover even if left alone by man (and there is no reason to believe that it will be left alone). The entire history of the whaling industry has been one of moving year after year into the harvesting of smaller and smaller species.

I suspect that as the world food shortage becomes more extreme, invasion of our territorial waters by an occasional Russian trawler and similar incidents will be replaced by a massive, no-holds-barred race to harvest the sea. Careful cropping—that is, the harvesting of only the surplus fishes so that the fisheries are not exhausted —seems even less likely to occur than it did in the whaling industry. With technological concentration on attaining a maximum harvest, it would not surprise me if the sea were virtually emptied of its fishes and shellfishes in a few decades or less. Whether or not the farming of tiny marine plants can then contribute significantly to our food supply remains to be seen. A lot would depend on how thoroughly we have poisoned the seas by that time.

What about some of the other panaceas, often highly touted in the public press? Certain food novelties have considerable potential—in the long run. For instance, protein-rich food can be produced by culturing microbes on petroleum, and it is theoretically possible that much, if not all, of the world's protein deficit over the next several decades could be made up from this source. But the project is still in its pilot stage. Large-scale acceptance trials have not been conducted. The economics of production and distribution have not been worked out. We do not know, for instance, how the product could be provided to people in the non-petroleum producing areas of the world, unless they had money to buy it. It is virtually axiomatic that the charity of the DCs can provide no real cure for the problems of the UDCs. We won't see substantial food from petroleum in time to have much effect in the next decade or so, and, since the petroleum supply is finite, it can be no long-range cure. But with extraordinary effort it might help to provide an interim solution.

Other ways of reducing the protein deficit are being actively promoted. Work is going ahead on the production of grains with higher quality proteins—those which contain a better balance of the protein building-blocks (amino acids) that are necessary for human nutrition. This is being done both by breeding new varieties and by fortifying grain grown from traditional varieties. New protein foods are being produced by adding oilseed protein concentrates to foods based on cereals. The best known of these is Incaparina, developed by INCAP (Institute of Nutrition for Central America and Panama). It is a mixture of corn and cottonseed meal enriched with vitamins A and B. Another is CSM formula (corn, soya, milk). It is a mixture of 70% processed corn, 25% soy protein concentrate, and 5% milk solids. A third is Vita-Soy, a high-protein beverage now being marketed in Hong Kong. All of these and related products should be viewed as future "hopes," not current cures. The economics of their production and distribution are not well worked out. And, more important, the question of their general acceptability remains open. Incaparina has been available in Central America for more than a decade, but its impact, to quote the Paddock brothers,[32] "remains insignificant." It remains insignificant in the face of determined efforts by private and commercial organizations to push its acceptance, and in spite of tremendous worldwide publicity. The Paddocks consider the principal problem to be its bland taste and texture. As they say, "The food tastes of a people are truly puzzling and as difficut to alter as their views on family planning."

Other unorthodox ways of providing more food are being discussed. These range from herding animals not presently being herded, such as the South American capybara (a rodent) and the African eland (an antelope), to the culturing of algae in the fecal slime of our sewerage treatment plants. To my knowledge, none of these is being attempted at the moment, nor is such development being seriously planned.

In my opinion, the current program with highest potential for reducing the scale of the coming famines involves the development and distribution of new high-yield varieties of food grains. Increasing the yield on land already under cultivation in this way is sociologically the easiest and ecologically the most intelligent method of "multiplying bread." New rice varieties, developed primarily at the International Rice Institute, may help lift rice production in the UDCs from the present 1,000 to 1,500 pounds per acre of rough rice toward the 4,000 to 6,000 pounds produced in the United States, Japan, Italy, and other DCs. Similar results may be hoped for with improved varieties of wheat and corn, many developed at the International Maize and Wheat Improvement Center in Mexico. All of these new grains have the potential for at least doubling yields under proper growing conditions. They are, for instance, much more responsive to fertilizer than older varieties.

Lester R. Brown, Administrator of the International Agricultural Development Service, reports[32] that an estimated 16 million acres were planted in new grain varieties in the 1967–1968 crop year. He considers it possible that the planting of these varieties may as much as double next year. Brown considers that "the overall trend [in production] will be up," but he also warns of problems:

"As improved seed becomes available, the new varieties are often quickly adopted by a relatively small group of farmers—the larger, more commercial farmers who have adequate irrigation and credit. But the irrigated land suitable to new varieties is limited. And in West Pakistan, for example, lack of farm credit is limiting the distribution of available fertilizer. But these difficulties should not be overestimated, since West Pakistan is expected to harvest a wheat crop this spring some 10% above the previous record.

"The rate of adoption may also be influenced by other factors. Extremely high prices for rice during the past year have stimulated interest in planting improved varieties. As output increases, prices may drop somewhat from present levels—reducing incentives to plant or carry out essential cultural practices. The increased output can also lead to problems with inadequate marketing facilities.

"Much land is not suited to the new varieties now being disseminated. Some farmers, after trying them, will return to traditional varieties."

Over all, Brown is extremely enthusiastic about the new varieties, hoping that they may cause an agricultural revolution in Asia. He feels they are playing a role as a catalyst, "causing farmers to break with tradition and reconsider their agricultural practices." I hope he is right. It will be a few years before really substantial estimates of the long-term value of the new varieties that have been rushed into production can be made. We do not know how they will do under field conditions over the long run—how resistant they will be to the attacks of pests. Recently William Paddock[34] has presented a plant pathologist's view of the crash programs to shift to new varieties. He describes India's dramatic program of planting improved Mexican wheat. Then he continues: "Such a rapid switch to a new variety is clearly understandable in a country that totters on the brink of famine. Yet with such limited testing, one wonders what unknown pathogens await a climatic change which will give the environmental conditions needed for their growth."

Again, the ecological problem: new varieties planted in denser populations, perhaps planted several times a year; simplified communities especially ripe for disaster; and, on top of this, ominous talk of more "inputs" of pesticides and fertilizers. We obviously are going to go ahead and take the great risks associated with the increased "inputs." We can only hope that the long-term balance will be positive. Meanwhile, until the new varieties accomplish their revolution, we would be wise to accept the more pessimistic estimates of UDC food production. We already know that it is impossible to increase food production enough to cope with continued population growth. No improvement of UDC food production can do more than delay the day of reckoning unless population control is successful.

Since success with both increasing productivity and controlling population is highly problematical, it would be foolish in the extreme to plan as if both would occur. As Housman said, "Train for ill and not for good."

Protecting Our Environment

Slowly but surely the more obvious aspects of environmental deterioration are beginning to register on Americans. After all, it is pretty hard to ignore the stench that exudes from most of our open bodies of water, or the tears streaming down our cheeks as we inhale the mixture of poisonous gases and solid particles that passes for air in many of our cities. Our newspapers are replete with stories on pollution and with plans to clean it up. We read of the appointment, by Secretary of the Interior Udall, of a new head of the Federal Water Pollution Control Administration. We read that ships sailing in Lake Erie are being urged by the Public Health Service not to use lake water taken within five miles of the U.S. coast for either drinking or cooking. The water is so full of filth and chemicals that not even boiling or chlorination will make it safe. We read that Dr. Merril Eisenbud, appointed by Mayor Lindsay as Environmental Director for New York City, has warned that pollution could destroy that city. A story in the Palo Alto *Times* was recently headlined: " 'Noise Pollution' Newest Unwanted Product of Civilization." Another bore the banner: "Clean Air, Water Possible at a Price." A five-part series in the same paper by AP science writer Alton Blakeslee was entitled: "A Fouled-up Planet." The last article in this series was headlined "Quick-Fix Remedies Ill-Considered." And so it goes: "U.S. and Industry Will Study Smog," "Cities Sharing Pollution Status," "Pollution Called Multiple Peril," "Aid Cuts May Peril Pollution Control," "Florida Orders Sewage Control," "Udall Bars Lowering of Water Pollution Standards," and "U.S. Faces Disaster Unless Air Pollution Controlled."

The burst of interest in pollution is not confined to the newspapers. Journals such as *Science, Scientific American,* and *New Scientist* also abound in articles on the subject: "Air Pollution: The 'Feds' Move to Abate Idaho Pulp Mill Stench," "The Control of Air Pollution," "Lake Tahoe: Measured for Pollution," "Pollution from Chimneys," "Synthetic Detergents: Their Influence Upon Iron-binding Complexes of Natural Waters," "Air Conservation Report Reflects National Concern," "Toxic Substances and Ecological Cycles," and "A Damaging Source of Air Pollution."

Clearly, one can no longer say that public attention has not been focused on the problems of pollution. Of course, focusing on the problems and doing something about them may be two

111

different things. Los Angeles, for instance, has had stringent smog control laws for about 20 years. Breathed any of their air lately? In Los Angeles and similar cities the human population has exceeded the carrying capacity of the environment—at least with respect to the ability of the atmosphere to remove waste. Unfortunately, Los Angeles smog laws have just barely been able to keep pace with their increasing population of automobiles (the main source of L.A. smog). And it seems unlikely that much improvement can be expected in this aspect of air pollution until a major shift in our economy takes place. As long as we have an automobile industry centered on the internal combustion engine, we are likely to remain in trouble. Certain of the contaminants (hydrocarbons) may be greatly eliminated by "afterburners." It remains to be seen whether an economical, desirable car can be produced that will eliminate all the serious contaminants, including the dangerous nitrogen oxides that are unaffected by the afterburners. Unless a lot more effort is put in on perfecting and producing devices to restrict smog output, our growing population of automobiles should keep Los Angeles and similar cities unfit for human habitation. The only *long-term* direction for the automobile industry, considering the finite nature of the petroleum supply, is to move to different sources of power, anyway.

In spite of the serious nature of industrial-automotive air pollution, it is perhaps the most easily solved of our pollution problems. Factories and automobiles can be forced to meet standards of pollutant production, and I suspect that in most cases this can be done without serious economic loss. Indeed, there are already many stories of industries that have profited by selling the materials that they once gaily disgorged into the atmosphere. The recovery devices have been more than paid for by the sales. But even if we must pay more for our automobiles, or get along with only one per family, or drive electric cars with miserable pickup, slow speed, and short range, these will be small prices for not rotting our lungs. The time "wasted" in driving slowly to the corner drugstore will be compensated by a smaller chance of being mangled before you get home, and by years of longevity tacked on to the end of your life. Think of the pleasure in living those extra years breathing clean air!

Pesticide pollution in the air and elsewhere may be more difficult to deal with. As I mentioned earlier, the immediate threat to your health from pesticides is not great. It is unlikely that you will drop dead of parathion poisoning tomorrow. We are much less sure, however, of the long-term effects of the many pesticides with which we are being constantly assailed. Tolerances to pesticides are set by the federal government, you say? Doesn't that protect us from their harmful effects? Hardly. First of all, most tolerances are set on the basis of short-term animal experiments and are set one poison at a time. Then, when it proves to be impossible to keep tolerances within limits, pressures are brought on the government, and the tolerances are conveniently raised. The original Food and Drug Administration (FDA) tolerances for DDT in milk fed to babies was zero. But now that virtually all milk is DDT contaminated, the FDA is going to set new tolerances.

The Rienows, in their superb book, *Moment in the Sun*,[35] describe the situation very well:

"What do all the thousands of 'minute, insignificant' tolerance-doses of chlorinated hydrocarbons, the antibiotics, organic phosphates, herbicides, hormones, systemic insecticides, rodenticides, fungicides, preservatives, arsenic additives, the omnipresent sodium nitrates and sodium nitrites, tranquilizer residues, coal tar colors, the emulsifiers, propionates, and possible carcinogens add up to in an average American's six-month diet, for instance?"

The answer is that in all probability they add up to plenty. But we'll never know for sure what the long-term effects are until the long term has passed. We won't even know then, unless the proper research programs are set up to study these effects of the various compounds, both alone and in various combinations. Studying them in combination is most important, since two compounds may act together (synergistically) in most unpleasant ways. For instance, there is growing evidence that inhaling asbestos fibers (a rather common air pollutant) and smoking cigarettes produce a greater possibility of developing lung cancer than the sum of the chances produced by asbestos or smoking, alone. My guess is that a certain portion of our high mortality rates from degenerative diseases can probably be assigned to the constant assault on our cells by small doses of biologically active chemicals. I would also not be surprised if some of the mysterious "viruses" individuals complain of were actually low-level poisonings. Remember the Romans!

Americans at least deserve to know what decisions are being made for them. Perhaps the benefits of many or most of these compounds are worth whatever the increased risks are, *but those risks must be made clear*. Unfortunately, governmental programs designed to evaluate the risks, establish tolerances, and enforce the rules are inadequate beyond belief. Look at the government's role in controlling how we and our environment are being dosed with powerful pesticides.

The Department of Agriculture (USDA) has had a long history of pushing pesticides, displaying a high level of ecological incompetence in the process. An outstanding example can be found in the history of the fire ant program. I'd like to discuss this program in some detail for two reasons. First, the action occurred long enough ago

115

so that the results are now clear. Second, I was personally involved in the controversy about the program.

The fire ant is a nasty but not-too-serious pest in the Southeastern United States. Its nests form mounds that interfere with the working of fields. Its stings may cause severe illness or death in sensitive people, but it is a considerably smaller menace in this regard than are bees and wasps. The ant is best described as a major nuisance. After limited and inadequate research on the biology of the fire ant, the USDA in 1957 came up with the astonishing idea of carrying out a massive aerial spray campaign against the ant. Along with other biologists, including those most familiar with the fire ant, I protested the planned program, pointing out, among other things, that the fire ant would be one of the *last* things seriously affected by a broadcast spray program. A quote from a letter I wrote concerning the problem to Ezra Taft Benson, then Secretary of Agriculture, follows:

"To any trained biologist a scorched-earth policy involving the treatment of twenty million acres with a highly potent poison such as dieldrin should be considered as a last-ditch stand, one resorted to only after all of the possible alternatives have been investigated. In addition, such a dangerous program should not even be considered unless the pest involved is an extremely serious threat to *life* and property.

116

"Is the Department of Agriculture aware that there are other consequences of such a program aside from the immediate death of vast numbers of animals? Is it aware that even poisoning the soil in a carefully planned strip system is bound to upset the ecological balance in the area? We are all too ignorant of the possible sequelae of such a program. Has it been pointed out that an adaptable and widespread organism such as the fire ant is one of the least likely of the insects in the treated area to be exterminated? It is also highly likely that, considering its large population size, the fire ant will have the reserve of genetic variability to permit the survival of resistant strains.

"I would strongly recommend that the program be suspended: (1) until the biology of the ant can be thoroughly investigated with a view toward biological control, baiting, or some other control method superior to broadcast poisoning. and (2) until trained ecologists can do the field studies necessary to give a reasonable evaluation of the chances of success, and the concomitant damage to the human population, wildlife, and the biotic community in general of *any* contemplated control program."

I received a reply from C. F. Curl, then Acting Director of the USDA Plant Pest Control Division. Note the emphasis on "eradication" in this excerpt:

"Surveys do indicate that the imported fire ant

infests approximately 20,000,000 acres in our Southern states. This does not mean, however, that the eradication program is embarked on a 'scorched-earth policy.' The infestation is not continuous, and the insecticide is applied only to areas where it is known to exist. The small outlying areas are being treated first to prevent further spread, and of the larger generally infested areas only a portion is treated in any one year.

"The method of eradication—namely, the application in granular form of two pounds of either dieldrin or heptachlor per acre—is based on an analysis of research information compiled from state and federal sources. Use experience on other control programs such as the white-fringed beetle and Japanese beetle was also taken into consideration before the final decisions were made. All the data indicated that a program could be developed which would be safe and would present a minimum of hazard to the ecological balance in the areas to be treated.

"To date, approximately 130,000 acres have been treated. This includes a block of 12,000 acres at El Dorado, Arkansas, treated nearly a year ago. Reports indicate the program is successful in eradicating the ants. No active mounds have been found in the El Dorado area, and the results look equally good in other locations treated to date. Observers vitally interested in the impact of this program to other forms of life have not reported serious disturbances to the area as a whole.

"Close liaison has been established with the Fish and Wildlife Service to continue their observations and to keep us informed currently as to the effect this program may have on fish and wildlife in the area. Experience to date indicates that a successful program can be carried out with a minimum hazard to the beneficial forms of life present.

"We believe that the points mentioned in your letter were given ample consideration before the initiation of the fire ant eradication program. We recognize, of course, that in any program where insecticides are used, certain precautions are necessary. Our experience has shown that insecticides can be applied successfully using very definite guidelines which can be established to minimize the hazard to fish and wildlife and to preclude any hazard to domestic animals and human health. Such guidelines are being followed in the operation of all control and eradication programs in which the U.S. Department of Agriculture participates."

In order to permit you to judge for yourself which one of us was right, let me quote to you parts of an article on the results of the program by Dr. William L. Brown, Jr., of the Department of Entomology of Cornell University. Dr. Brown, an outstanding biologist and a world authority on ants, wrote:[36]

"With astonishing swiftness, and over the mounting protests of conservation and other groups alarmed at the prospect of another airborne 'spray' program, the first insecticides were laid down in November, 1957. The rate of application was two pounds of dieldrin or heptachlor per acre. . . . Dieldrin and heptachlor are extremely toxic substances—about 4 to 15 times as toxic to wildlife as is DDT. Many wildlife experts and conservationists, as well as entomologists both basic and economic, felt a sense of foreboding at the start of a program that would deposit poisons with 8 to 30 times the killing power of the common forest dosage of DDT (one pound per acre in gypsy moth control).

". . . The misgivings of the wildlife people seem to have been justified on the whole, since the kill of wildlife in sample treated areas appears to have been high in most of those that have been adequately checked. The USDA disputes many of the claims of damage, but their own statements often tend to be vague and general.

". . . Although the USDA claims that the evidence is inconclusive in some cases, there does exist contrary information indicating that stock losses from fire ant poisons may sometimes be significant.

". . . A serious blow was dealt the program in late 1958, when treatments were only one year old; Senator Sparkman and Congressman Boykin of Alabama asked that the fire ant campaign be suspended until the benefits and dangers could be evaluated properly. Then, in the beginning of 1960, the Food and Drug Administration of the Department of Health, Education, and Welfare lowered the tolerance for heptachlor residues on harvested crops to zero, following the discovery that heptachlor was transformed by weathering into a persistent and highly toxic derivative, heptachlor epoxide, residues of which turn up in meat and milk when fed to stock. Some state entomologists now definitely advise farmers against the use of heptachlor on pasture or forage.

". . . The original plan set forth in 1957 called for eradication of the ant on the North American continent, by rolling back the infestation from its borders, applying eradication measures to more central foci in the main infestation, and instituting an effective program of treatment of especially dangerous sources of spread, such as nurseries. Nearly four years and perhaps fifteen million dollars after that plan was announced, the fire ant is still turning up in new counties, and is being rediscovered in counties thought to have been freed of the pest in Arkansas, Louisiana, Florida, and North Carolina."

This rather lengthy discussion should give you some insight into two of the government agencies that should be most active in preserving the quality of our environment. The USDA, against the advice of the most competent people in the field, launched a fruitless eradication campaign which could have positive results only for the stock-holders of pesticide companies. The FDA discovered another of its tolerance levels was established at the wrong level. How many of today's tolerance levels do you suppose are mis-set?

Lest you be left with the impression that the USDA is manned only by ecological incompetents, let me in fairness point out that some of the most ecologically sophisticated pest control programs have been initiated by the Department. Perhaps the most brilliant was that against the screwworm, a fly which can be an extremely serious pest on cattle. Annual losses in livestock have been estimated to be as high as $40 million a year. Under the leadership of Dr. E. F. Knipling, the USDA embarked on a massive program of sterilizing male screwworm flies and releasing them in infested areas. The female screwworm mates only once. By flooding infested areas with sterile males, the screwworm was effectively eradicated from the United States. The effectiveness of this "biological control" program makes an interesting contrast with the futile and destructive fire ant fiasco.

At the moment I am afraid that, rather than protecting our environment from deterioration, the USDA still, in the balance, is furthering that deterioration. It is still much too ready to yield to the pressures to take the chemical quick way out, to keep food esthetically appealing instead of poison-free. The setting of tolerances by the FDA is much too open to error (as can be seen by repeated readjustments), and the power available to enforce tolerances is completely inadequate. Less than one-third of 1% of the produce that you eat has been subject to federal inspection for pesticide residues, and even that small portion may well have been coated, post-inspection, by overzealous storekeepers trying to discourage flies in their supermarkets. I well remember being warned years ago by an economic entomologist employed by the State of Kansas not to eat asparagus one year. It turned out that the farmers were spraying far beyond the official tolerances, knowing that the chances of being caught were practically nil. Such occurrences are not rare and will not become rare until adequate inspection systems are established.

The only description of current laws and programs designed to restore our national open sewer systems to the status of rivers and lakes is that they are inadequate in the extreme. In the past decade or so concern has increased, and some influential people have been pushing in the right direction. These people include President Johnson and Stewart Udall, Secretary of the Interior. But the greed and stubbornness of industries, the recalcitrance of city governments, the weakness of state control agencies, and the general apathy of the American people have combined to keep progress discouragingly slow.

What the government is up against in trying to

get some industries to stop destroying our country is described in detail by reporter Frank Graham, Jr., in his fine book *Disaster by Default*.[37] Particularly instructive is the story of the great Mississippi fish kill in the early 1960's. Rough estimates give the total loss in the four years 1960–1963 as between 10 and 15 million fishes in the lower Mississippi and its bypass, the Atchafalaya.[38] The fishes killed included several kinds of catfishes, menhaden, mullet, sea trout, drum, shad, and buffalo. The die-offs were ruinous to the local fishing industry. A thorough investigation by government (Public Health Service) and private laboratories placed the blame primarily on the highly toxic insecticide endrin and one of its derivatives. It was found not only in the blood and tissues of dying fishes and water birds, but also in the mud in areas where fishes were dying. Extracts made both from the mud and from the tissues of dying fishes killed healthy fishes in experiments. Fish kills were greatest in 1960 and 1963, smallest in 1961 and 1962. Endrin was used commonly to treat cotton and cane fields in the lower Mississippi Valley in 1960 and 1963; very little was used in 1961 and 1962.

The finger of the Public Health Service pointed to waste from the Velsicol Chemical Corporation's Memphis plant as one major source of the endrin, the other being run-off from agricultural lands following dusting and spraying. Waste endrin from the manufacturing process was getting into the river. The reaction of the Velsicol Corporation should come as no surprise. Graham in *Disaster by Default*[39] described the action:

"Velsicol, under fire, shot back. Bernard Lorant, the company's vice-president in charge of research, issued strong denials. In a statement to the press, he said that endrin had nothing to do with the Mississippi fish kill, that the symptoms of the dying fish were not those of endrin poisoning, and that Velsicol's tests proved that the fish had died of dropsy."

"Dropsy"—isn't that quaint! All you tropical fish fanciers can check that one out. Turn to page 61 of your copy of William T. Innes's *Exotic Aquarium Fishes* (19th Edition), edited by Professor George S. Myers, one of the world's most renowned experts on fishes. Under "Dropsy" we read: "The puzzling thing about the malady is the unaccountable way in which it singles out individual fishes. It is *never epidemic*." (My emphasis.) Add to this the facts cited above, and the small point that the fishes had the symptoms of endrin poisoning, and we have a great natural miracle. By coincidence, perhaps ten million fishes simultaneously contracted a new form of dropsy with the symptoms of endrin poisoning. In order to fool investigators they produced endrin in their tissues and excreted it into the mud of the Mississippi. Let's just hope that the approximately one million humans who drink that heady Mississippi brew don't come down in future years with a new form of "dropsy," which is delayed in its appearance and tries to fool you by having the symptoms of cirrhosis of the liver.

At a 1964 conference on the fish kill, a common theme promoted by our giants of the pesticide industry was very much in evidence: that only Communist sympathizers criticize the way pesticides are thrown around. This approach is exemplified by a statement (quoted by Graham) made well before the conference by Parke C. Brinkley, president of the National Agricultural Chemicals Association:

"Two of the biggest battles in this war [against Communism] are the battle against starvation and the battle against disease. No two things make people more ripe for Communism. The most effective tool in the hands of the farmer and in the hands of the public health official as they fight these battles is pesticides."

A reading of Graham's fine book will quickly unite you with the fishermen of Mississippi, the dwellers on the shores of "Sewer Erie," and many others in the belief that the American people have powerful enemies in addition to the Communists.

The story is depressingly the same across the nation. The struggles of the government over a decade to get cooperation from cities and slaughterhouses on the Missouri River to abate the hideous pollution of the river with blood, guts, hair, and "paunch manure" (undigested stomach contents) are a typical example. In 1957 Omaha city officials said they would cooperate. In 1965 the city was still dumping 300,000 pounds of untreated paunch manure and quantities of grease into the river. Sewage pollution in Raritan Bay, New Jersey, concentrated by clams, led to an epidemic of hepatitis. The clamming industry in the Bay was closed down. Tough luck for the clammers. Tough luck for those who like to eat clams. Very tough luck for those who did and contracted hepatitis. No one protects the rights of fishermen, swimmers, or just the poor benighted souls who don't like the stink and slime. But then perhaps nothing in our Constitution guarantees our senses protection from loathsome assault.

The story of industrial pollution in Lake Michigan, of sewage pollution in the Hudson, and of acid pollution in Pennsylvania streams by strip miners reads much the same. Some small progress has been made in pollution abatement, but overall the situation is still going downhill. One important move has been in forcing detergent manufacturers to switch to chemicals that can be more readily broken down by natural processes than were previous ingredients. Even that problem has not been solved, however. Although the new compounds seem to break down in commercial sewage treatment facilities, they still create problems in septic tanks.

The war against another kind of pollution deserves mention here: noise pollution. It is getting considerable attention from the designers of dwellings, factories, and office buildings, but not as much attention as it should be getting. And the sources of noise—the motorcycles, power mowers, jet transports, TV sets, trucks, and so forth—multiply merrily on with the population. There is considerable evidence that excessive noise levels are harmful in a number of ways, including a permanent hearing loss after long exposure. We're about to cross a new threshold in deafening horror if the Federal Aviation Administration and a small segment of the aircraft and airline industries are permitted to proceed with their preposterous supersonic transport (SST) project. I am a pilot. I have lots of friends who are pilots, including airline pilots. I've yet to run into one who thinks that the SST is sensible or necessary.

Aviation has colossal needs. It needs improved airports with adequate runways and clear approaches, located far enough from major cities so that dangerous noise abatement procedures can be dispensed with. At some airports these procedures require reducing power at a critical stage of takeoff in order to protect the ears and sleep of people living nearby. Aviation also needs fast, convenient ground transport to these terminals, and improved air traffic control procedures. It needs just about everything except airplanes which, if operated over the continent, will subject Americans to a shocking succession of sonic booms. It needs just about everything except airplanes that will deposit their contrails so high in the atmosphere that they will lie above the layers of air which are regularly mixed, and thus will persist. The SST represents a beautiful example of the runaway stupidity that can characterize the end of a technological trend. A major criterion of a good airplane has in the past almost always been how fast it can fly. After the SST we'll doubtless move on to orbital transports that will circle the earth before reentering, cutting the time from the Mojave Desert to Cape Kennedy to a mere hour (Los Angeles–New York will probably remain from five to six hours even then). It is quite a measure of our civilization that in order to save a few people an hour or so in crossing the country we would subject millions to extreme disturbance and property damage—to say nothing of possibly contributing significantly to environmental catastrophe.

Resistance to the SST is forming, however. For instance, Karl M. Ruppenthal, Transworld Airlines pilot who is director of the transportation management program of the Graduate School of Business at Stanford University, recently condemned the entire project. He points out that with 175 SSTs flying our domestic air routes, people living along those routes would be subjected to 700 booms a day—a boom on the average of every two minutes or so. Every two minutes a sound as loud as that made by a modern subsonic jet as it lifts off the runway under full power, passing right over your head, will interrupt your daily routine. Maybe, with luck, we can destroy this monster before it gets off the ground. If not, it would be smart to buy stock in a company selling ear plugs.

What, then, is being done overall to nurse our sick environment back to health? How well are we treating these symptoms of the Earth's disease of overpopulation? Are we getting ahead of the filth, corruption, and noise? Are we guarding the natural cycles on which our lives depend? Are we protecting ourselves from subtle and chronic poisoning? The answer is obvious—the palliatives are too few and too weak. The patient continues to get sicker.

CHAPTER 4

WHAT NEEDS TO BE DONE

A general answer to the question, "What needs to be done?" is simple. We must rapidly bring the world population under control, reducing the growth rate to zero or making it go negative. Conscious regulation of human numbers must be achieved. Simultaneously we must, at least temporarily, greatly increase our food production. This agricultural program should be carefully monitored to minimize deleterious effects on the environment and should include an effective program of ecosystem restoration. As these projects are carried out, an international policy research program must be initiated to set optimum population-environment goals for the world and to devise methods for reaching these goals. So the answer to the question is simple. Getting the job done, unfortunately, is going to be complex beyond belief—if indeed it can be done. What follows in this chapter are some ideas on how these goals *might* be reached and a brief assessment of our chances of reaching them.

Getting Our House in Order

The key to the whole business, in my opinion, is held by the United States. We are the most influential superpower; we are the richest nation in the world. At the same time we are also just one country on an ever-shrinking planet. It is obvious that we cannot exist unaffected by the fate of our fellows on the other end of the good ship Earth. If their end of the ship sinks, we shall at the very least have to put up with the spectacle of their drowning and listen to their screams. Communications satellites guarantee that we will be treated to the sights and sounds of mass starvation on the evening news, just as we now can see Viet Cong corpses being disposed of in living color and listen to the groans of our own wounded. We're unlikely, however, to get off with just our appetites spoiled and our consciences disturbed. We are going to be sitting on top of the only food surpluses available for distribution, and those surpluses will not be large. In addition, it is not unreasonable to expect our level of affluence to continue to increase over the next few years as the situation in the rest of the world grows ever more desperate. Can we guess what effect this growing disparity will have on our "shipmates" in the UDCs? Will they starve gracefully, without rocking the boat? Or will they attempt to overwhelm us in order to get what they consider to be their fair share?

We, of course, cannot remain affluent and isolated. At the moment the United States uses well over half of all the raw materials consumed each year. Think of it. Less than 1/15th of the population of the world requires more than all the rest to maintain its inflated position. If present trends continue, in 20 years we will be much less than 1/15th of the population, and yet we may use some 80% of the resources consumed. Our affluence depends heavily on many different kinds of imports: ferroalloys (metals used to make various kinds of steel), tin, bauxite (aluminum ore), rubber, and so forth. Will other countries, many of them in the grip of starvation and anarchy, still happily supply these materials to a nation that cannot give them food? Even the technological optimists don't think we can free ourselves of the need for imports in the near future, so we're going to be up against it. But, then, at least our balance of payments should improve!

So, beside our own serious population problem at home, we are intimately involved in the world crisis. We are involved through our import-export situation. We are involved because of the

133

possibilities of global ecological catastrophe, of global pestilence, and of global thermonuclear war. Also, we are involved because of the humanitarian feelings of most Americans.

We are going to face some extremely difficult but unavoidable decisions. By how much, and at what environmental risk, should we increase our food production in an attempt to feed the starving? How much should we reduce the grain-finishing of beef in order to have more food for export? How will we react when asked to balance the lives of a million Latin Americans against, say, a 30 cent per pound rise in the average price of beef? Will we be willing to slaughter our dogs and cats in order to divert pet food protein to the starving masses in Asia? If these choices are presented one at a time, out of context, I predict that our behavior will be "selfish." Men do not seem to be able to focus emotionally on distant or long-term events. Immediacy seems to be necessary to elicit "selfless" responses. Few Americans could sit in the same room with a child and watch it starve to death. But the death of several million children this year from starvation is a distant, impersonal, hard-to-grasp event. You will note that I put quotes around "selfish" and "selfless." The words describe the behavior only out of context. The "selfless" actions necessary to aid the rest of the world and stabilize the population are our only hope for survival. The "selfish" ones work only toward our destruction. Ways must be found to bring home to all the American people the reality of the threat to their way of life—indeed to their very lives.

Obviously our first step must be to immediately establish and advertise drastic policies designed to bring our own population size under control. We must define a goal of a stable optimum population size for the United States and display our determination to move rapidly toward that goal. Such a move does two things at once. It improves our chances of obtaining the kind of country and society we all want, and it sets an example for the world. The second step is very important, as we also are going to have to adopt some very tough foreign policy positions relative to population control, and we must do it from a psychologically strong position. We will want to disarm one group of opponents at the outset: those who claim that we wish others to stop breeding while we go merrily ahead. We want our propaganda based on "do as we do"—not "do as we say."

So the first task is population control at home. How do we go about it? Many of my colleagues feel that some sort of compulsory birth regulation would be necessary to achieve such control. One plan often mentioned involves the addition of temporary sterilants to water supplies or staple food. Doses of the antidote would be carefully rationed by the government to produce the desired population size. Those of you who are appalled at such a suggestion can rest easy. The option isn't even open to us, thanks to the criminal inadequacy of biomedical research in this area. If the choice now is either such additives or catastrophe, we shall have catastrophe. It might be possible to develop such population control tools, although the task would not be simple. Either the additive would have to operate equally well and with minimum side effects against both sexes, or some way would have to be found to direct it only to one sex and shield the other. Feeding potent male hormones to the whole population might sterilize and defeminize the women, while the upset in the male population and society as a whole can be well imagined. In addition, care would have to be taken to see to it that the sterilizing substance did not reach livestock, either through water or garbage.

Technical problems aside, I suspect you'll agree with me that society would probably dissolve before sterilants were added to the water supply by the government. Just consider the fluoridation controversy! Some other way will have to be found. Perhaps the most workable system would be to reverse the government's present system of encouraging reproduction and replace it with a series of financial rewards and penalties designed to discourage reproduction. For instance, we could reverse our present system of tax exemptions. Since taxes in essence purchase services from the government and since large families require more services, why not make them pay for them? The present system was designed at a time when larger population size was not viewed as undesirable. But no sane society wants to promote larger population size today. The new system would be quite simple (but, of course, not retroactive!). For each of the first two children, an additional $600 would be added to the "taxable income" figure from which the taxes are calculated. For each subsequent child, $1,200 would be added. In order to prevent hardship, minimum levels would be established guaranteeing each family enough for food, clothing, and shelter. Therefore a family with three children and only $4,000 income might pay little or no taxes, but parents making $25,000 who had ten children would pay for their reproductive irresponsibility by forking over the taxes on $35,800. In short, the plush life would be difficult to attain for those with large families—which is as it should be, since they are getting their pleasure from their children, who are being supported in part by more responsible members of society.

On top of the income tax reversal, luxury taxes should be placed on layettes, cribs, diapers, diaper services, expensive toys, always with the proviso that the essentials be available without penalty to the poor (just as free food now is). There would, of course, have to be considerable experimenting on the level of financial pressure necessary to achieve the population goals. To the penalties could be added some incentives. A governmental "first marriage grant" could be awarded each couple in which the age of both partners was 25 or more. "Responsibility prizes" could be given to each couple for each five years of childless marriage, or to each man who accepted irreversible sterilization (vasectomy) before having more than two children. Or special lotteries might be held—tickets going only to the childless. Adoption could be subsidized and made a simple procedure. Considering the savings in school buildings, pollution control, unemployment compensation, and the like, these grants would be a money-making proposition. But even if they weren't, the price would be a small one to pay for saving our nation.

Obviously, such measures would need coordination by a powerful governmental agency. A federal Department of Population and Environment (DPE) should be set up with the power to take whatever steps are necessary to establish a reasonable population size in the United States and to put an end to the steady deterioration of our environment. The DPE would be given ample funds to support research in the areas of population control and environmental quality. In the first area it would promote intensive investigation of new techniques of birth control, possibly leading to the development of mass sterilizing agents such as were discussed above. This research will not only give us better methods to use at home; they are absolutely essential if we are to help the UDCs to control their populations. Many peoples lack the incentive to use the Pill. A program requiring daily attention just will not work. This is one reason why a Papal decision to accept the Pill but not other methods of birth control would be only a small step in the right direction. The DPE also would encourage more research on human sex determination, for if a simple method could be found to guarantee that first-born children were males, then population control problems in many areas would be somewhat eased. In our country and elsewhere couples with only female children "keep trying" in hope of a son.

Two other functions of the DPE would be to aid Congress in developing legislation relating to population and environment, and to inform the public of the needs for such legislation. Some of these needs are already apparent. We need a federal law guaranteeing the right of *any* woman to have an abortion if it is approved by a physician. We need federal legislation guaranteeing the right to voluntary sterilization for both sexes and protecting physicians who perform such operations from legal harassment. We need a federal law requiring sex education in schools—sex education that includes discussion of the need for regulating the birth rate and of the techniques of birth control. Such education should begin at the earliest age recommended by those

139

with professional competence in this area—certainly before junior high school.

By "sex education" I do not mean courses focusing on hygiene or presenting a simple-minded "birds and bees" approach to human sexuality. The reproductive function of sex must be shown as just one of its functions, and one that must be carefully regulated in relation to the needs of the individual and society. Much emphasis must be placed on sex as an interpersonal relationship, as an important and extremely pleasurable aspect of being human, as mankind's major and most enduring recreation, as a fountainhead of his humor, as a phenomenon that affects every aspect of his being. Contrary to popular mythology, sex is one of man's *least* "animal" functions. First of all, many animals (and plants) get along without any sex whatsoever. They reproduce asexually. It is clear from biological research that sex is not primarily a mechanism of reproduction; it is a mechanism that promotes variability. In many organisms which do have sexual processes, these processes occur at a stage in the life cycle that is not the stage at which reproduction occurs. And, of course, no other animal has all of the vast cultural ramifications of sex that have developed in human society. In short, sex, as we know it, *is a peculiarly human activity*. It has many complex functions other than the production of offspring. It is now imperative that we restrict the reproductive function of sex while producing a minimum of disruption in the others.

Fortunately, there are hopeful signs that the anti-human notions that have long kept Western society in a state of sexual repression no longer hold sway over many of our citizens. With a rational atmosphere mankind should be able to work out the problems of de-emphasizing the reproductive role of sex. These problems include finding substitutes for the sexual satisfaction which many women derive from childbearing and finding substitutes for the ego satisfaction that often accompanies excessive fatherhood. A rational atmosphere should also make it easier to deal with the problems of venereal disease and of illegitimacy. The role of marriage would become one of providing the proper environment for the rearing of wanted children. All too often today marriage either provides a "license" for sexual activity or a way of legitimizing the results of premarital sexual activity.

If we take the proper steps in education, legislation, and research, we should be able in a generation to have a population thoroughly enjoying its sexual activity, while raising smaller numbers of physically and mentally healthier children. The population should be relatively free of the horrors created today by divorce, illegal abortion, venereal disease, and the psychological pressures of a sexually repressive and repressed society. Much, of course, needs to be done, but support for action in these directions is becoming more and more common in the medical profession, the clergy, and the public at large. If present trends can be continued, we should be able to minimize and in some cases reverse social pressures against population control at home and to influence those abroad in the same direction.

Of course, this enlightened atmosphere does not exist today. Potent forces still must be overcome if we are to get the attitude of our government changed in the area of population control. Although the performance and attitudes of American Catholics relative to the use of birth control are similar to those of non-Catholics, conservative elements in the Church hierarchy still resist change. The degree to which this resistance goes against the attitudes of American Catholics was revealed in a Gallup Poll taken in late 1965. Of the Catholics questioned, 56 percent expressed the opinion that the Church should change its opinion on methods of birth control, while only 33 percent thought it should not change. Opinion among intellectual Catholics seems even more heavily in favor of a change in the Church's position.

Recently Pope Paul VI formed a commission to study in detail the question of birth control. The majority opinion of this commission was that the practice of birth control by means other than those involving abortion was wholly consistent with the Catholic view of marriage and sexuality, and that the method of birth control to be used can best be decided by the couple concerned. This opinion, the commission felt, fit directly into the teaching on responsible parenthood of the Second Vatican Council.

Since this report should have dissolved any fears the Pope may have had about contraception, it is a mystery to informed Catholics why he has not acted.

A Catholic colleague, Dr. John H. Thomas, recently wrote to me, "My first duty as a Catholic is to do what I believe is morally correct. There is no doubt in my mind that the position of the Church with respect to birth control is morally wrong. The price of doctrinaire insistence on unworkable methods of birth control is high. It contributes to misery and starvation for billions, and perhaps the end of civilization as we know it. As a scientist I also know that Catholic doctrine in this area is without biological foundation. It is therefore my duty both to myself and to the Church not just to ignore this doctrine, but to do everything within my power to change it. After all, without drastic worldwide measures for population control in the near future, there will be no Church anyway. If the Church, or, for that matter, any organized religion, is to survive, it must become much more humanitarian in focus. If it does, the theology will take care of itself."

All these are hopeful signs, but unhappily the Church hierarchy and certain conservative Catholic groups are still hard at work to raise the death rate by fighting *effective* moves to lower the birth rate. It takes a great deal of patience for a biologist familiar with the miseries of overpopulation to read through documents that represent the views of even "enlightened" Catholics. For instance, consider the views of Dr. Donald N. Barrett, Professor of Sociology at Notre Dame. Married and the father of ten children, Dr. Barrett testified before Senator Gruening's Subcommittee on March 2, 1966.[40] The testimony was given on a bill to coordinate and disseminate birth control information upon request. Dr. Barrett makes the strong point that action in population control must avoid government coercion (he makes the distinction that the Catholic Church in this matter is only "morally coercive"). He is unwilling to cooperate with any group which supports abortion or sterilization as birth control methods. He puts much weight on refinements of the rhythm method, which is patently hopeless as a population control method. Much emphasis is put on "licit" methods. The "moral coercion" of the Church is present in veiled threats to the Subcommittee not to take positions that would prevent a consensus acceptable to the Catholic Church. Barrett's testimony was notably free of comment on the physical coerciveness of starvation, plague, and thermonuclear war. Nor does he comment on the human values that will be lost when civilization goes down the drain. I wonder what Barrett thinks of his Church's role in keeping help, in the form of contraceptive education and devices, from those miserable people in Colombia. How hollow his talk of "moral coercion" would sound down there! You might note that if Barrett's descendants continued his rate of propagation for just ten generations, they would number in the tenth generation ten billion people—three times the entire population of the Earth today.

The testimony of William H. Ball, general counsel for the Pennsylvania Catholic Conference, before Senator Gruening's committee[41] also makes interesting, if depressing, reading. Its tenor can be guessed by a quote from Ball's article in *Commonweal*[42] entitled "The Court and Birth Control." He states in that article that the government "should be neutral, neither penalizing birth control nor promoting it." In his testimony he expresses great concern for "freedom from governmental inquisition, the related right of privacy, concern for the weaker members of society," and "governmental coercion of mind and conscience." Curiously, though, he does not discuss the great increase in governmental interference and restriction of freedom that has accompanied population growth. He does not mention what has been happening to privacy as population increases. He does not talk about protecting the poor of the world from starvation that is a

145

direct result of population pressure. Let me quote the phrases from his testimony that most thoroughly attest to the total absurdity of his view:

"The repetition of the term 'population' throughout the text, the reference in the bill to population 'control,' *coupled with an absence of any indication of means other than population control as a solution to problems of population growth.* . . ." (My emphasis.) It will hardly come as a shock to you that he says a little further on, "At the time when the Congress contemplates embarking the nation upon so unprecedented a program, the Pennsylvania Catholic Conference feels it its duty to state its conviction that the public power and public funds should not be used for the providing of birth control services."

In short, Catholic witnesses are opposed even to attempts to institute inadequate federal programs of population control. Catholic politicians at home and abroad operate in many ways to obstruct population control. They often effectively block action on population control at the international level. And population control, of course, is the *only* solution to problems of population growth. Unless the Pope does a complete about-face, I think we can count on continuing and effective Catholic support for raising the death rate.

This encouragement of high death rates through political interference is now the most important role of the Church in the population crisis. There is little reason to believe that, if obstructionist behavior by the hierarchy and other influential Catholics ceased, *performance* of Catholic couples would differ significantly from that of non-Catholics in most areas. Furthermore, in the UDCs outside of Latin America Catholics are rarely a significant portion of the problem. It is a mistake to focus too strongly on the Catholic element in the population situation. True, we must bring pressure to bear on the Pope in hope of getting a reversal of the Church's position. Probably the best way is to support those American Catholics who already realize that opposition to birth control is automatically support for increased misery and death. If such a reversal can be obtained, mankind's chances for survival will improve somewhat, and millions upon millions of Catholics will be able to lead better lives. But the population problem will not be "solved."

Biologists must promote understanding of the facts of reproductive biology which relate to matters of abortion and contraception. They must do more than simply reiterate the facts of population dynamics. They must point out the biological absurdity of equating a zygote (the cell created by joining of sperm and egg) or fetus (unborn child) with a human being. As Professor Garret Hardin of the University of California pointed out, that is like confusing a set of blueprints with a building. People are people because of the interaction of genetic information (stored in a chemical language) with an environment. Clearly, the most "humanizing" element of that environment is the cultural element, to which the child is not exposed until after birth. When conception is prevented or a fetus destroyed, the *potential* for another human being is lost, but that is all. That potential is lost *regardless* of the reason that conception does not occur—there is no biological difference if the egg is not fertilized because of timing, or because of mechanical or other interference.

Biologists must point out that contraception is for many reasons more desirable than abortion. But they must also point out that in many cases abortion is much more desirable than childbirth. Above all, biologists must take the side of the hungry billions of *living* human beings today and tomorrow, not the side of *potential* human beings. Remember, unless numbers are limited, if those potential human beings are born, they will at best lead miserable lives and die young. We cannot permit the destruction of humanity to be abetted by a doctrine conceived in total ignorance of the biological facts of life.

Basically, I think the Catholic situation is much more amenable to solution than that associated with our current views of economics. The winds of change are clearly blowing in religion —blowing too late, perhaps, but blowing. Yet the idea of an ever-expanding economy fueled by population growth seems tightly entrenched in the minds of businessmen, if not in the minds of economists. Each new baby is viewed as a consumer to stimulate an ever-growing economy. Each baby is, of course, potentially one of the unemployed, but a consumer nonetheless. The Rienows[43] estimate that each American baby will consume in a 70-year life span, directly or indirectly: 26 million gallons of water, 21 thousand gallons of gasoline, 10 thousand pounds of meat, 28 thousand pounds of milk and cream, $5,000 to $8,000 in school building materials, $6,300 worth of clothing, and $7,000 worth of furniture. It's not a baby, it's Superconsumer!

Our entire economy is geared to growing population and monumental waste. Buy land and hold it; the price is sure to go up. Why? Exploding population on a finite planet. Buy natural resources stocks; their price is sure to go up. Why? Exploding population and finite resources. Buy automotive or airline stocks; their price is sure to go up. Why? More people to move around. Buy baby food stocks; their price is sure to go up. Why? You guess. And so it goes. Up goes the population and up goes that magical figure, the Gross National Product (GNP). And, as anyone who takes a close look at the glut, waste, pollution, and ugliness of America today can testify, it is well-named—as *gross* a product as one could wish for. We have assumed the role

149

of the robber barons of all time. We have decided that we are the chosen people to steal all we can get of our planet's gradually stored and limited resources. To hell with future generations, and to hell with our fellow human beings today! We'll fly high now—hopefully they'll pay later.

We thought the game would end only in hundreds or even thousands of years through resource depletion. But the bill is coming due before we expected it. Now we find that to be among the least of our problems. The poor of the world show signs of not being happy with our position. Indeed even the poor at home seem a little ill-disposed toward our behavior. Maybe we can hold them down by force, you say. Maybe so—that remains to be seen. It is likely to be uneconomical to do so. Besides, what has been properly called "the *effluent* society" shows signs of strangling itself without the intervention of enraged "have-nots." Will our gross national product soon be reduced to no national product?

The answer is that it surely will unless we take a hard look at our present economic system. There are some very distinguished economists who do not feel that our capitalist system must be fueled by an ever-growing population or ever-continuing depletion of resources (both of which are impossible, anyway). There, in fact, seems to be no reason why the GNP cannot be kept growing for a very long time *without population growth*.

Dr. J. J. Spengler recently wrote,[44] "In the future, economic growth will depend mainly upon invention, innovation, technical progress, and capital formation, upon institutionalized growth-favoring arrangements. Population growth will probably play an even smaller role than I have assigned it in earlier discussion. *It is high time, therefore, that business cease looking upon the stork as a bird of good omen.*" (My emphasis.)

Ways must be found to promote the idea that problems associated with population growth will more than cancel the "advantages" of financial prosperity. Perhaps the best way to do this would be to encourage Americans to ask exactly what our financial prosperity is for. What will be done with leisure time and money when all vacation spots are crowded beyond belief? Is it worth living in the Los Angeles smog for 50 weeks in order to spend two weeks in Yosemite Valley—when the Valley in the summer may be even more crowded than L.A. and twice as smoggy? What good is having the money for a fishing trip when fish are dead or poisonous because of pesticide pollution? Why own a fancy car in which to get asphyxiated in monster traffic jams? Do we want more and more of the same until we have destroyed ourselves? Sizable segments of our population, especially the young, are already answering that question: "Hell, no!" Their response should be considered carefully by population-promoting tycoons.

Obviously, the problem of our deteriorating environment is tied in very closely with the over-all economic problem. We must reverse the attitudes so beautifully exemplified by one of our giants of industry when he said that "the ability of a river to absorb sewage is one of our great natural resources and should be utilized to the utmost."[45] Legal steps must be taken, and taken fast, to see to it that polluters pay through the nose for their destructive acts. The old idea that industry could create the mess and then the taxpayers must clean it up has to go. The garbage produced by an industry is the responsibility of that industry. The government should not use other people's money to clean it up. Keep the government out of business. Let it play its proper role in a capitalistic society—seeing to it that all segments of private enterprise do business honestly, seeing to it that the interests of the fishing industry are not subordinated to those of the petrochemical industry, seeing to it that your right to swim in a public lake is not subordinated to the desire of a steel company to make an inflated profit.

The policeman against environmental deterioration must be the powerful Department of Population and Environment mentioned above. It must be carefully insulated against the forces that will quickly be aligned against it. It is going to cost industry money. It is going to cost municipalities money. It is going to hit a lot of us where it hurts. We may have to do without two gas-gulping monster cars per family. We may have to learn to get along with some insect damage in our produce. We may have to get along with much less fancy packaging of the goods we purchase. We may have to use cleaners that get our clothes something less than "whiter than white." We may have to be satisfied with slower coast-to-coast transportation. Such may be the cost of survival. Of course, we may also have to get along with less emphysema, less cancer, less heart disease, less noise, less filth, less crowding, less need to work long hours or "moonlight," less robbery, less assault, less murder, and less threat of war. The pace of life may slow down. We may have more fishing, more relaxing, more time to watch TV, more time to drink beer (served in bottles that *must* be returned).

The Department of Population and Environment (DPE) would place extremely strict controls on the use of dangerous pesticides and would encourage research on economically more reasonable methods of control. We have barely scratched the surface in what can be done with biological controls, including ways of manipulating the genetics of populations. We do not know enough about the ways the chemical and biological controls might be integrated in ecologically intelligent ways. But perhaps the greatest service the DPE might perform immediately from its inception would be to expose the stupidity and futility of today's pesticide practices. Any properly constituted DPE would have a strong complement of systems ecologists—ecologists who use the methods of operations research and systems analysis to evaluate complex ecological systems. As a foretaste of what the DPE might say, let me quote to you from a letter I recently received from Professor K. E. F. Watt of the University of California, one of today's outstanding systems ecologists:

". . . most control programs are set up without a threshold; that is, spray is used each season whether significant densities of pests are present or not. Thus, this is an example of a business providing the amazing spectacle of supporting an overhead which is not associated with a corresponding marginal increase in gross profit. It is this type of practice which has led many fruit orchard owners into such dire economic straits that they have had to sell their land for housing projects or factory sites.

"It is most important to point out to the public that a pest control program should have two consequences: (1) either plant or animal being attacked by the pests should be saved, and (2) there should be fewer pests in subsequent generations following treatment. The yardstick by which all control programs should be evaluated comes from those dramatically successful programs in which plants or animals were saved, and pests declined in density. You are aware of examples that provide this yardstick . . . the Florida screwworm study is a prize example. *By this criterion most pesticide projects have been failures.*" (My emphasis.)

The DPE would also be responsible for pushing legislation to stop the wasting of resources. It would move toward creating a vast waste recovery industry, an industry that might well make "trash' obsolete. Reusable containers might be required by law for virtually all products, as was recently suggested by Dr. Athelstan Spilhaus.[46] He points out the necessity of controlling trash and pollutants at the source, stating, "Regardless of what any economist tells me, I'm convinced by the second law of thermodynamics that it must be cheaper to collect something at the source than to scrape it off the buildings, wash it out of the clothes, and so forth." There's that old, immutable law again. If the product is deteriorated and scattered, usable energy has been lost, and more must be injected into the system if order is to be restored, by either collecting or reconstituting the product. The less deterioration or scattering we permit, the less energy we must use. And energy is expensive.

The DPE would have to take a good hard look at our energy budget, especially at the rate at which we are expending our irreplaceable fossil fuels. It would have to evaluate carefully the possible role of atomic fission or fusion in replacing fossil fuels as an energy source. It would have to evaluate hydroelectric power in relation to the other two. These sources cannot be considered in isolation. Atomic facilities must have their waste disposal problems integrated into the evaluation. Hydroelectric power must be considered in a framework of the gradual altering of the ecology of rivers and flood plains and of Earth's topography through the building and silting up of dams. It must be considered in relationship to salmon fisheries and downstream farming. Both atomic and hydroelectric power must be considered in relation to the expenditures of fossil fuels required to mine, transport, and process the metals and concrete from which facilities are built. That we are presently living beyond our means is obvious from the simple fact that we are madly depleting nonreplenishable resources. Careful plans must be laid for getting the Earth back in balance, on the hopeful assumption that some way can be found to avoid the doom now confronting us.

By now you are probably fed up with this discussion. Americans will do none of these things, you say. Well, I'm inclined to agree. As an eternal optimist, however, I will provide some suggestions in the last chapter of this book for what you might do to improve the chances that action will be taken. Improve them from, say, one in a thousand to one in a hundred, but improve them. Meanwhile let's make the unlikely assumption that this country will turn aside from its suicidal course and start a sensible domestic program of population and environmental control. How can we then help with the world problem?

Realism and International Aid

Once the United States has adopted sane policies at home, we will be in a position to take the lead in finding a solution to the problem on a world scale. What we will need first and foremost is a plan that will produce a maximum amelioration of the time of famines with the relatively limited resources we have in hand. Even drastic population control measures need decades to work, and we do not have the capacity to feed the needy of the world over the next decade or so. Our giant food surpluses are gone, and even at maximum production we would not be able to produce surplus enough for all (to say nothing of getting it properly distributed). In addition, we are the only country which will be in a position to give away food. Canada, Australia, Argentina, and the other few countries with exportable surpluses will be largely occupied with selling food to hungry countries that are in a position to pay. These granary countries will need the income that they earn in this way, or the goods they can receive in exchange for food. The

UDCs cannot expect major charity from them.

What kind of policies should we be designing to guide our actions during the time of famines? To my knowledge, there has been only one realistic suggestion in this area—a policy proposed by William and Paul Paddock in their book *Famine—1975!* The Paddocks suggest an American policy based on the concept of "triage" borrowed from military medicine. The idea briefly is this: When casualties crowd a dressing station to the point where all cannot be cared for by the limited medical staff, some decisions must be made on who will be treated. For this purpose the triage system of classification was developed. All incoming casualties are placed in one of three classes. In the first class are those who will die regardless of treatment. In the second are those who will survive regardless of treatment. The third contains those who can be saved only if they are given prompt treatment. When medical aid is limited, it is concentrated only on the third group—the others are left untreated.

The Paddocks suggest that we devise a similar system for classifying nations. Some will undergo the transition to self-sufficiency without drastic aid from us. They will be ones with abundant money for foreign purchases, or with efficient governments, strong population control programs, and strong agricultural development programs. Although our aid might help them, they could get along without it. The Paddocks suggest that Libya is probably such a country. It has the resources, in the form of oil, that will allow it to purchase food as its population booms. If analysis shows them to be correct, we should withhold food aid from Libya.

Some nations, on the other hand, may become self-sufficient if we give them help. They have a chance to make it if we can give them some food to tide them over. The Paddocks think that Pakistan, at least West Pakistan, may be such a country. Others to whom I have spoken agree. Our food aid may give the Pakistani government, under the tough-minded leadership of President Ayub Khan, time to press home its population control and agricultural development programs. If they are right, we should continue to ship food to Pakistan.

Finally there is the last tragic category—those countries that are so far behind in the population-food game that there is no hope that our food aid will see them through to self-sufficiency. The Paddocks say that India is probably in this category. If it is, then under the triage system she should receive no more food.

The Paddocks' views have not, to say the least, been greeted with enthusiasm by the Indian government. Nor have their views been applauded by those in our government whose jobs depend on the willy-nilly spreading of American largess abroad, or by the assorted do-gooders who are deeply involved in the apparatus of international food charity. India, as we noted earlier, blames its current problems on bad monsoons (which indeed did occur). It has conveniently forgotten that the Indian government itself predicted in 1959 that a serious, gap would appear between food production and population in 1965–1966. At any rate, the Indian government seems deeply concerned about the possibility that the Paddocks' idea might take hold and that India will be denied further food.

In my opinion, there is no rational choice *except* to adopt some form of the Paddocks' strategy as far as food distribution is concerned. I have incorporated a version of it in a broader plan I am suggesting below. The Paddocks deserve immense credit for their courage and foresight in publishing *Famine—1975!*, which may be remembered as one of the most important books of our age. They will receive criticism from certain segments of our society. They will offend the groups which discounted the warnings of a decade or more ago, warnings that we would be in serious trouble today unless the population was brought under control. Criticism from those groups is a compliment.

What might be a possible strategy leading to man's passage with minimum casualties through the time of famines? Obviously, if we are to find a long-range solution, the full weight of the resources of the United States and the other DCs must be brought to bear. My suggestion would be that the United States, Russia, Great Britain, Canada, Japan, Australia, Europe, and other DCs immediately set up, through the United Nations, a machinery for "area rehabilitation." This plan would involve simultaneous population control, agricultural development, and, where resources warrant it, industrialization of selected countries or sections of countries. The bedrock requirement of this program would be population control, necessarily including migration control to prevent swamping of aided areas by the less fortunate. Of course, the size of the areas covered would be dependent in no small part on the scale and effectiveness of the effort made by the developed countries. Hopefully, we can persuade the United States to lead the way. So far our efforts toward aiding the UDCs have, in terms of the percentage of our gross national product committed, been behind that of many other DCs, who can less well afford it.

The specific requirements of the program would vary from area to area. Possibly the first step in all areas would be to set up relay stations and distribute small transistorized TV sets to villages for communal viewing of satellite-transmitted programs. We must have channels for reaching the largely rural populations of the "other world." TV programs would explain the rehabilitation plan for each area. These programs would have to be produced with the combined skill of Madison Avenue, of people with great expertise in the subjects to be presented, and of people with intimate knowledge of the target population. The programs could be presented both "straight" and as cleverly devised "entertainment." They would introduce the UDC populations to the need for agricultural innovations and explain public health measures. The programs would use the prospect of increased affluence as a major incentive for gaining cooperation. It seems unlikely that the threat of future starvation would have much impact. If necessary, however, the TV channel could be used to make it clear that the continuance of food supplies depends on the cooperation of the people in the area. Perhaps they could be made to realize that only by making progress toward population control and self-sufficiency can they avoid disaster.

Other steps would vary a great deal from place to place. In some agricultural areas needs would be well enough known for assistance to start immediately, perhaps with "on site" training of agricultural technicians. Such a program could lead to a sort of "county agricultural agent" system in which trained people work closely with farmers. These systems have proved their great worth in many parts of the world. Schools to train agents and other agricultural personnel, including farmers brought in on rotation, would be of immense value to the agriculture of most UDCs.

In some places the problems of agriculture would be so severe that research stations, manned by teams from the DCs, might have to function for a decade or so before local agriculture had a chance of being revolutionized. "Improved" strains of various crops developed elsewhere might not grow satisfactorily or might be unacceptable to the local people as food. Since the supply of trained people in DCs suitable for running stations doing research in exotic agriculture is limited, priority systems for station establishment must be set up. At the same time ways must be found to increase the supply of agricultural scientists being trained in the DCs.

In all areas studies should be initiated to determine how much agricultural and industrial development is feasible. Demographers must determine how many people, at each stage of development, can live reasonably comfortable, secure lives. That is, demographic goals must be set that are reasonable in the light of each country's basic resources. Unless demographic goals are set and met, the entire program will inevitably fail. Population control must be made to work, or all our other efforts will have been in vain.

Needless to say, the sociopolitical problems of initiating such a program would be colossal. It might not, for instance, be feasible to operate through the United Nations, because countries will not all be aided equally. This problem might be sidestepped by using the "area" concept rather than strictly political units. Thus, if migration could be controlled, some sections of India might be aided and others not. Perhaps we should support secessionist movements in UDCs when the group departing is better developed than the previous political unit as a whole. Perhaps we should have supported Katanga, not the Congo. Perhaps we should now support Biafra, not Nigeria. West Pakistan might receive aid, but not East Pakistan. It might be to our advantage to have some UDCs more divided or even rearranged, especially along economic axes. After all, most political boundaries in Southern Asia and Africa reflect not economically viable units, but the conflicting interests of European powers 75 years ago. I know this all sounds very callous, but remember the alternative. The callous acts have long since been committed by those who over the years have obstructed a birth rate solution or downgraded or ignored the entire problem. Now the time has come to pay the piper, and the same kind of obstructionists remain. If they succeed, we will all go down the drain.

While we are working toward setting up a world program of the general sort outlined above, the United States could take effective unilateral action in many cases. A good example of how we might have acted can be built around the Chandrasekhar incident I mentioned earlier. When he suggested sterilizing all Indian males with three or more children, we should have applied pressure on the Indian government to go ahead with the plan. We should have volunteered logistic support in the form of helicopters, vehicles, and surgical instruments. We should have sent doctors to aid in the program by setting up centers for training para-medical personnel to do vasectomies. Coercion? Perhaps, but coercion in a good cause. I am sometimes astounded at the attitudes of Americans who are horrified at the prospect of our government insisting on population control as the price of food aid. All too often the very same people are fully in support of applying military force against those who disagree with our form of government or our foreign policy. We must be relentless in pushing for population control around the world.

I wish I could offer you some sugarcoated solutions, but I'm afraid the time for them is long gone. A cancer is an uncontrolled multiplication of cells; the population explosion is an uncontrolled multiplication of people. Treating only the symptoms of cancer may make the victim more comfortable at first, but eventually he dies—often horribly. A similar fate awaits a world with a population explosion if only the symptoms are treated. We must shift our efforts from treatment of the symptoms to the cutting out of the cancer. The operation will demand many apparently brutal and heartless decisions. The pain may be intense. But the disease is so far advanced that only with radical surgery does the patient have a chance of survival.

So far I have talked primarily about the strategy for easing us through the hazardous times ahead. But what of our ultimate goals? That, of course, is something that needs a great deal of discussion in the United States and elsewhere. Obviously, we need a stable world population with its size rationally controlled by society. But what should the size of that population be? What is the optimum number of human beings that the Earth can support? This is an extremely complex question. It involves value judgments about how crowded we should be. It also includes technical questions of how crowded we *can* be. Research should obviously be initiated in both areas immediately.

If we are to decide how crowded we should be, we must know a great deal more about man's perception of crowding and about how crowding affects human beings. Certainly people in different cultures and subcultures have different views of what densities of people (people per unit area) constitute crowding under different conditions. But what exactly are those densities and conditions? Under what conditions do people consider themselves neither crowded nor lonely? Research on these questions has barely been started. It must be accompanied by studies of how crowding affects people, including both "overcrowding" (too many people per unit area) and "un-

167

dercrowding" (too few per unit area). These problems are more difficult to study, especially since the effects of crowding are often confounded by poverty, poor diet, unattractive surroundings, and other related phenomena.

But difficult as these problems are, they must be investigated. We know all too well that when rats or other animals are overcrowded, the results are pronounced and usually unpleasant. Social systems may break down, cannibalism may occur, breeding may cease altogether. The results do not bode well for human beings as they get more and more crowded. But extrapolating from the behavior of rats to the behavior of human beings is much more risky than extrapolating from the physiology of rats to the physiology of human beings. Man's physical characteristics are much more ratlike than are his social systems. This research must be done on man.

Within the limits imposed by nature, I would view an optimum population size for the Earth to be one permitting any individual to be as crowded or as alone as he or she wished. Enough people should be present so that large cities are possible, but people should not be so numerous as to prevent people who so desire from being hermits. Pretty idealistic, but not impossible in theory. Besides, some pretty far-reaching changes are going to be required in human society over the next few decades, regardless of whether or not we stop the population explosion. We've already reached a density at which many of our institutions no longer function properly. As the distinguished historian, Walter Prescott Webb, pointed out 16 years ago,[47] with the closing of the World Frontier, a set of basic institutions and attitudes became outdated. When the Western Hemisphere was opened to exploitation by Europeans, a crowded condition suddenly was converted into an uncrowded one. In 1500 the ratio of people to available land in Europe was estimated to have been about 27 people per square mile. The addition of the vast, virtually unpopulated frontier of the New World moved this ratio back down to less than five per square mile. As Webb said, the frontier was, in essence, "a vast body of wealth without proprietors." Europeans moved rapidly to exploit the spatial, mineral, and other material wealth of the New World. They created an unprecedented economic boom that lasted some 400 years. The boom is clearly over, however, at least as far as land is concerned. The man/land ratio went beyond 27 people per square mile again before 1930. Since all of the material things on which the boom depended also come ultimately from the land, the entire boom is also clearly limited. Of course, how to end that boom gracefully, without the most fantastic "bust" of all time, is what this book is all about.

Somehow we've got to change from a growth-oriented, exploitative system to one focused on stability and conservation. Our entire system of orienting to nature must undergo a revolution. And that revolution is going to be extremely difficult to pull off, since the attitudes of Western culture toward nature are deeply rooted in Judeo-Christian tradition. Unlike people in many other cultures, we see man's basic role as that of dominating nature, rather than as living in harmony with it. This entire problem has been elegantly discussed by Professor Lynn White, Jr., in *Science* magazine.[48] He points out, for instance, that before the Christian era trees, springs, hills, streams, and other objects of nature had guardian spirits. These spirits had to be approached and placated before one could safely invade their territory. As White says, "By destroying pagan animism, Christianity made it possible to exploit nature in a mood of indifference to the feelings of natural objects." Christianity fostered the wide spread of basic ideas of "progress" and of time as something linear, nonrepeating, and absolute, flowing from the future into the past. Such ideas were foreign to the Greeks and Romans, who had a cyclical (repeating) view of time and could not envision the world as having a beginning. Although a modern physicist's view of time might be somewhat closer to that of the Greeks than the Christians, it is obvious that the Christian view is the one held by most of us. God designed and started the whole business for our benefit. He made a world for us to dominate and exploit. Our European ancestors had long since developed the "proper" attitudes when the opportunity to exploit the New World appeared.

Both science and technology can clearly be seen to have their historical roots in natural theology and the Christian dogma of man's rightful mastery over nature. Therefore, as White claims, it is probably in vain that so many look to science and technology to solve our present ecological crisis. Much more basic changes are needed, perhaps of the type exemplified by the much-despised "hippie" movement—a movement that adopts most of its religious ideas from the non-Christian East. It is a movement wrapped up in Zen Buddhism, physical love, and a disdain for material wealth. It is small wonder that our society is horrified at hippies' behavior—it goes against our most cherished religious and ethical ideas. I think it would be well if those of us who are totally ensnared in the non-hip part of our culture paid a great deal of attention to the movement, rather than condemn it out of hand. They may not have *the* answer, but they may have *an* answer. At the very least they are asking the proper questions. Here is what White, a churchman, has to say: "Both our present science and our present technology are so tinctured with orthodox Christian arrogance toward nature that no solution for our ecologic crisis can be expected from them alone. Since the roots of our trouble are so largely religious, the remedy must

171

also be essentially religious, whether we call it that or not."

So there is considerable reason for believing that extremely fundamental changes in our society are going to be required in order to preserve any semblance of the world we know. Furthermore, those changes are going to have to take place in a framework of certain natural limits. For, as I hope I have convinced you, even though we would like to dominate nature, it still dominates us!

What are those limits that are imposed by nature? We don't know exactly. Finding out will involve complex questions of energy sources and the availability of the materials necessary for the production of food. There is some disagreement as to exactly how dependent upon fossil fuels we shall remain and what the ultimate consequences of their depletion beyond certain levels will be. But at a minimum it seems safe to say that a population of one or even two billion people could be sustained in reasonable comfort for perhaps 1,000 years if resources were husbanded carefully. A mere century of stability should provide ample time to investigate most technological leads and to do the social adjusting and policy planning necessary to set realistic goals on a more or less permanent basis. Our big problem today is how to bring the population under control, reduce its size to that general range, and create the atmosphere in which necessary changes, investigations, and planning can take place. If we are not successful in reducing the population size, but do stabilize it at perhaps four or five billion, we will still have a chance. Of course, mankind's options will be fewer and people's lives almost certainly less pleasant than if the lower figure is attained.

The Chances of Success

Many of you are doubtless saying now, "It's too unrealistic—it can't be done." I think you're probably right—as I said earlier, the chances of success are small. Indeed, they are probably infinitesimal if success is to be measured only by the initiation of a complete program such as I have suggested. But partial programs can help. Indeed, even if the worst happens, short of the end of civilization, efforts toward solving the population problem may not be in vain. Suppose we do not prevent massive famines. Suppose there are widespread plagues. Suppose a billion people perish. At least if we have called enough attention to the problem, we may be able to keep the whole mess from recycling. We must make it impossible for people to blame the calamity on too little food or technological failures or "acts of God." They must at least face the essential cause of the problem—overpopulation.

CHAPTER 5

WHAT CAN YOU DO?

The question I am most frequently asked after giving talks about the population explosion is, "What can I do to help?" The obvious first answer is, "Set an example—don't have more than two children." That reply really sets the pace, because I am becoming more and more convinced that the only real hope in this crisis lies in the grass-roots activities of individuals. We must change public opinion in this country, and through public opinion change the direction of our government. The fact that we cannot count on vast funds to support our efforts does not have to be an insurmountable obstacle. In the five years that I have been a part-time propagandist, I have found that many people in influential positions share my concern. I have had encouraging letters from all over the world. People in radio and television have been extremely helpful in providing exposure for the issues. Exposure for the issues, however, is not enough. We must create enough pressure to convince politicians that their political survival is at stake unless they get behind some really effective measures to deal with mankind's most pressing problem. Now for some concrete suggestions of what you can do.

Writing Letters

Do not underestimate the power of the letter in the eyes of politicians and others in positions of power. Just think of the effect on our politics if every Senator and Representative received 100 different, intelligent letters every day, demanding action on the population explosion. In case you don't know who your Senators are or who your Representative is, you can find out by calling your public library. Sample letters to a Senator and a Representative are included in the appendix. Do not, of course, copy these. Make up your own, based on this book or on some of those listed in the bibliography. Try to confine your comments to a single page. For your convenience, here is a brief checklist of points you might want to make:

1. Population is far outstripping food production.
2. More than half of the world is hungry; many are dying of starvation.
3. Population growth must come to an end.

4. Our only choices are a lower birth rate or a bigger death rate.

5. Long-term growth rate must be zero.

6. It is necessary to plan for a stable population of optimum size.

7. Family planning alone does not lead to population control.

8. Change of attitudes is more important than contraceptive technology in population control.

9. Need for better contraceptive methods is great, notwithstanding (8).

10. In short term the only feasible way to increase food production greatly is by increasing yield on land already under production.

11. Research in tropical ecology and agriculture is badly needed.

12. Firm agricultural base is prerequisite for industrialization.

13. Not all countries can be industrialized.

14. DCs cannot feed UDCs.

15. Environmental deterioration poses a colossal threat to man's survival.

16. Governmental attention to this entire problem is less than insignificant.

Obviously even this partial list covers more points than one could reasonably make in a single letter. Try to develop a few of them and use follow-up letters to develop others. Try to connect letters to politicians with local projects and problems in which you know they are interested. If they come from the shores of the Great Lakes, mention the role population pressures are playing in the destruction of those lakes. If they come from Los Angeles, point out that the smog may be caused by too many cars, but that too many cars are caused by too many people. If the politicians you address are concerned with conservation, point out that conservation is a losing game without population control.

Letters may, of course, be written to state and local officials as well. These, too, would best focus on local issues. If a member of a local government is opposing needed school bonds, point out that his efforts would be more socially constructive if he were promoting population control. Fewer kids require fewer schools. If a state representative wants to destroy a park in order to build a freeway, point out that, if he had promoted population control in the past, the freeway might be made unnecessary. Bombard with mail any elected official who opposes liberalizing abortion laws.

Editors of magazines and newspapers are excellent targets for letters. Complain bitterly about any positive treatment of large families. Attack the publicizing of "mothers of the year" unless they have no more than two children or have adopted the extra ones. Request that the publications you address stop carrying any advertising implying by statement or inference that it is socially acceptable to have more than two children. Point out that any promotion of the idea that a growing population means prosperity is making a contribution to the destruction of America. Television and radio stations should be subjected to similar constant pressure. Series featuring large families should be assailed. More programming about the population crisis should be demanded. Ask for prime time programs on sex education and the use of contraceptives. Raise a fuss whenever programming or commercials promote reproductive irresponsibility. Ask for programs that expose our disgraceful laws regulating abortion and contraception. A letter to a television station is included in the appendix as one example of what you might write.

Another target for your letters is the business community, including chambers of commerce. Those producing offensive advertisements or advertising during offensive television programs should be threatened with boycott. Be tough: "Dear Sir: Your company's advertisement was shown in the middle of *The Sturdley Family,* implying your sponsorship of that program. The day is upon us when we can no longer tolerate television programs that feature large families as if they still represented acceptable behavior on the part of parents. I will never buy another of your franistans until . . ." Chambers of commerce are especially "black hat" on matters of population, and should be called down whenever they step out of line.

Finally, if you are a Catholic, you should let your Church know that you strongly disapprove of its policies on birth control. You can withdraw your financial support from the diocese and channel it into liberal Catholic causes. Remember that any organized religion is also a political organization and therefore responsive to grassroots pressure. The Church has survived for almost two millenia by adjusting, under pressure, to the times. You can help it survive by pressuring it to change. Indeed, if you belong to any religious or charitable organization that has as one goal the treatment of the symptoms of overpopulation, you should make it clear to the organization that its policies are not geared to realities. An example of two responsible Catholics' approaches to their Church is given in the appendix, along with a letter written by a Lutheran to the head of his Church.

You can surely think of other people to whom writing such letters would be helpful. Above all, if you really want to survive, start writing! Just think, if only 30,000 concerned people wrote one letter a day, the Establishment would be inundated with ten million letters a year. It will take effort and tenacity. But consider what will happen if we don't do it!

Organizing Action Groups

The time has come for us to assemble small groups of dedicated people who do not want to see our way of life destroyed by the population explosion. Feel lonely while writing your letter-a-day? Get a few like-minded friends together, form a group, and hold a letter-writing party once a week. Put together a blacklist of people, companies, and organizations impeding population control (or promoting environmental deterioration) and go to work on them. Organize boycotts of products of guilty companies. Work for the opponents of guilty politicians. Help each other write speeches and have the most vocal members of your group present them at PTAs, service clubs, or anywhere else you can get an audience. Telephone in to "talk shows" on radio or television and start discussions on population control. If sex education in your school system is inadequate (it is in almost all), educate yourself and start classes for the children in your group. Give your child an IUD to take to "show and tell." Above all, *raise a stink*. Let other people know how serious your group thinks the problem is and how determined you are to do something about it.

How much can be accomplished as a group will depend a great deal on how much enthusiasm for action you can generate and maintain. Some difficulty will be encountered in disagreement over exact steps to be taken, but if your goal is kept clearly in mind, this should be minimal.

Positive Reinforcement

So far I've concentrated on the attack. A great
deal of good can be done by encouraging those
who are moving in the right direction. People
like Senator Gruening and Secretary Udall like
to know that their efforts are appreciated, too.
If a politician makes a sensible statement on the
population problem, write him immediately and
praise him, and if he represents you, assure him
of your vote. If he takes a strong stand on the
problem, do volunteer work for him. Help him
get reelected by a landslide. Of course, the same
goes for business as a whole and the communications industry in general. When they move in the
right direction, let them hear about it. If a beer
company pays a reward for returning empty cans
(as Coors once did) switch to that brand—and
write the president of the company to tell him
you're doing it. When a TV show points up the
problems of overpopulation, write a letter of
thanks to the station.

Proselytizing Friends and Associates

At no small risk of being considered a nut, you can do a lot of good by persuading your personal acquaintances that the crisis is here, that something must be done, and that they can help. What follows are some specific suggestions for arguments that may help in certain circumstances. They are classified on the basis of a target individual.

TARGET ALREADY HAS EIGHT KIDS. Emphasize that the need for family limitation was not obvious before. Point out that target surely would not behave that way today. Target should now encourage others to "do as I say," not "do as I did." Remind him that if his children follow his example, he'll have 64 grandchildren to buy Christmas and birthday presents for.

TARGET IS CHILDLESS. Emphasize that target is paying through the nose to raise other people's children. Praise target for selfless devotion to mankind (even if you suspect target is sterile). Target should encourage others to "do as I do."

TARGET HAS TWO CHILDREN. Suggest that two

is plenty. If more are desired, suggest adoption. Point out that if target really loves children, more good can be done by adopting a child who has already been born. Target will have the pleasure of rearing the child, the child will have a good home. If target decides to have further children, point out that target is doing it for personal satisfaction, not out of love of children.

TARGET IS EXTREME CONSERVATIVE. Point out that overpopulation breeds conditions in which communism and "big government" thrive. Explain that larger numbers weaken, not strengthen, the United States. Report that Russia and China have realized this and are moving to limit their populations. Remind target that the United States fought World War II with a population of less than 150 million people, and that future wars will depend more on firepower than manpower.

TARGET IS EXTREME LIBERAL. Emphasize that the rich are getting richer and the poor poorer, both in the United States and in the world as a whole. Declare that as long as population continues to grow, this disparity will worsen, and the goal of a "fair deal" for all will recede.

TARGET IS A DEEPLY RELIGIOUS CATHOLIC. Cite support of religious leaders of *all* faiths for the need to limit populations. Point out that it is only a question of technique of birth control that divides the Catholic Church today. Show target Dr. Thomas's statement in Chapter IV and his letter and that of Dr. Parnell in the appendix to indicate how informed Catholic opinion differs with hierarchy. Quote to target from Dr. M. H. Mothersill's book *Birth Control and Conscience*: "There are religious leaders today in the twentieth century who strain at the gnat of artificial contraception and then swallow the camel of overpopulation, poverty, famine, crime, and the conditions which lead to war. Then they say, 'Peace, Peace!' when by their outdated pronationalism they have induced conditions such that there can be no peace!"

TARGET SAYS THERE IS AN "INALIENABLE RIGHT" TO HAVE AS MANY CHILDREN AS ONE WANTS. Point out that as long as the invention of inalienable rights is in vogue, you've invented a few of your own. They are:

1. The right to limit our families.
2. The right to eat.
3. The right to eat meat.
4. The right to drink pure water.
5. The right to live uncrowded.
6. The right to avoid regimentation.
7. The right to hunt and fish.
8. The right to view natural beauty.
9. The right to breathe clean air.
10. The right to silence.
11. The right to avoid pesticide poisoning.
12. The right to be free of thermonuclear war.
13. The right to educate our children.

187

14. The right to have grandchildren.
15. The right to have great-grandchildren.

Since the price of having all these "inalienable rights" is giving up the right to irresponsible reproduction, you win 15 "rights" to one.

TARGET BRINGS UP QUESTIONS OF EUGENICS—SHOULDN'T SOME PEOPLE BREED AND OTHERS BE STERILIZED? This is an old routine—basically target is saying, "My superior kind should breed, yours should abstain for the good of mankind." Some targets may be concerned, for instance, with possible degeneration of human intelligence to overbreeding of the "less smart." Quote me as a specialist on genetic changes in populations to the effect that:

1. Intelligence in man has both genetic and environmental components. You might think of each individual as having an inherited possible range of intelligence. His or her environment—diet, home life, schooling—determine what level within that range is actually achieved. This is an oversimplification, but it is close enough.

2. If, over perhaps five generations, those at the lower end of the genetic intelligence scale far outbred those at the upper end, the average I.Q. in the population could be expected to be reduced by a few points.

3. If such a change were detected, aver-

age I.Q. could be returned to its previous level by the proper breeding program—that is, the change would be reversible.

4. There is no evidence that any such drastic differential in breeding exists.

5. It is critical that we start reducing the number of people in this generation—worrying about genetic effects over the next four to five generations would be pointless even if we detected a differential today.

6. Anyone really concerned with raising the level of intelligence in our population should fight to raise the environmental component. We *know* that drastic increases can be made in one generation by improved home and school situations and in some cases by improved diet.

7. Most geneticists feel that if the genetic component of human intelligence is to be manipulated in the future, it is likely to be dealt with biochemically by treating individuals. Huge selective breeding programs on populations present many technical, social, and political difficulties.

8. Research *is* being done on the estimation of the genetic component of variance in quantitative characters like intelligence, but to date we have not come close to solving the genetic problems of determining an individual's intellectual endowment. Even more importantly, we have not solved the

problems of cross-cultural I.Q. testing. When we can do those things, we will easily be able to ask the question whether tall people are genetically smarter than short people, or whether black people may be smarter than white people. The results would be of some very limited academic interest to biologists and sociologists. For instance, environmental deprivation may have created strong selection for genetic intelligence in black populations, so that the average genetic I.Q. of Negroes might be a few points higher than that of the white population. It is clear from evidence on other similar genetic characters that no two samples of *Homo sapiens* would be identical with respect to genetic intelligence. A sample of Swedes would differ from a sample of Englishmen. A sample of carpenters would differ from a sample of plumbers. Tall people would differ from short people, and two different samples of tall Anglo-Saxon Protestants would differ from each other. It is also clear that any social action on genetic intelligence would be taken on the basis of that characteristic in an individual, and not on the basis of height, eye color, skin color, tooth size, blood type, or the like. For instance, once you knew each child's genetic intelligence, you would use this, not skin color or hair type, to judge his or her educational potential. Thus the claim that studies of genetic I.Q. in a context of skin color are biologically or sociologically important is absolute and utter nonsense. Clearly, the genetic quality question is a red herring and should be kept out of our action program for the next generation.

TARGET IS UNIVERSITY PROFESSOR. Chances are your target will be intellectually convinced that there is a problem. In all probability, however, he will be unable to take action because his training and current environment all militate *against* action. His idea of "action" is to form a committee or to urge "more research." Both courses are actually substitutes for action. Neither will do much good in the crisis we face now. We've got lots of committees, and decades ago enough research had been done at least to outline the problem and make clear many of the steps necessary to solve it. Unless those steps are taken, research initiated today will be terminated not by success but by the problem under investigation. It is unwise for people in the woods downwind from a roaring forest fire to sit down and start research on new-methods of fire fighting or on techniques of reforestation—unless a very able and adequate crew is already combating the blaze with whatever methods are already available.

You must convince the professor that he should

immediately use his influence in every way possible within and outside of the university to get the fire crews on the line. The population crisis must be an integral part of his teaching—it is pertinent to *every* subject. He must use the prestige of his position in writing letters to whomever he thinks he can influence most. If he is in English or drama, he may be able to write novels or plays emphasizing near-future worlds in which famines or plagues are changing the very nature of mankind and his societies. If he is in business school, he can "hit the road" lecturing to business groups and industrial conferences on "The Stork as an Enemy of Capitalism." If he is in the physical sciences, he can write strong letters to his narrow-minded colleagues who are proposing idiotic panaceas to solve the food problem. Any scientist can be urged to write to the *Scientific American* and similar journals to ask the editors to stop accepting advertisements that imply that a technology for mining or farming the sea can save humanity. The high standards that these journals maintain in their articles should also apply to their advertising. Scientists who serve on government committees can be pressed to exploit their position to awaken our sleeping government. Any professor, lecturing anywhere, can insert into his lecture a "commercial" on the problem. "And so I come to the end of my discussion of the literary significance of Darwin's hangnail. In conclusion, I would like to remind

192

you that our Society for the Study of Darwin's Hangnail can only exist in a world in which there is leisure time for intellectual pursuits, and a social system which permits such pursuits. Unless something is done *now* to bring the runaway human population under control, the SSDH will not long endure."

Within his university, the professor can be urged to help pave the way for the momentous changes that are certain to rock society and the medieval structure of his institution as the population explosion comes to a halt. Whatever stops the explosion, it is clear that today's deteriorating educational system will be shaken from top to bottom. Universities are already under assault from politicians. They are facing a wave of ideas and protests from students and are in competition with "free universities" designed and operating under entirely new assumptions. If we survive the crisis, new methods of teaching are in most cases going to replace the 50-minute lecture. New subjects are being added now, so there will be a strong trend toward deleting many old ones. Patchwork departmental structures are going to go, as will much of today's emphasis on tests and grading. *If* we get through the crisis, universities, like the Catholic Church, will evolve or die. But before we can find out which, we must first get through the crisis.

TARGET IS A SCHOOLTEACHER. It will be easy for you to convince most schoolteachers that the population problem is *very real*. They have been struggling with overcrowded classrooms and ghetto children for a long time. They see first-hand the inability of our society to provide a proper environment for its major product—children. Recommending action to schoolteachers is another problem. They are under the thumb of school boards that all too often are opposed to the teaching of anything socially important in school. Race relations, sex, politics, religion are all "too controversial." Those subjects should be "taught at home." The parents of the children are, of course, usually hopelessly incompetent to teach any of these subjects. Why shouldn't they be? After all, they were educated by the very same school system. But this doesn't bother the school boards. They were never taught to think through a problem. They had reading, writing, arithmetic, and social studies just like Grandpa. Between the teacher and the school board stand the school administrators. The motto of most school administrators is simple: "Don't make waves."

So unless your teacher friend is one of the fortunate few in really first-rate educational systems or institutions, any determined public action inside or outside of school will probably just cost him his job. Subtle propaganda to the kiddies and letter writing is about all you can ask for. But do ask for that.

TARGET IS A "DOVE." A very large segment of

our population is deeply committed to an anti-war stance, as well they should be. But they are to some extent concentrating on just one more symptom of the disease of overpopulation. Population pressures promote wars, whether the pressures are real or simply imagined. When Pope Urban II preached the First Crusade in November, 1095, he referred to the advantages of gaining new lands. Indeed, as Professor D. L. Bilderback, a historian at Fresno State College, recently pointed out to me, the "First Crusade was made up largely of second sons who were dispossessed by the increasing European attachment to primogeniture (inheritance by the first-born son)." There is also evidence of considerable effort in 15th-century Europe in activities such as land reclamation. Things seem to have been getting pretty crowded and difficult for Europeans just before the opening of the New World frontier. Needless to say, the expanding, exploiting swarms of Europeans fought wars, not only among themselves, but against the small native populations, as they scrambled over the newly available territories.

In more recent history we have the stunning example of Nazi Germany's drive for "Lebensraum" (territory for expansion) and Japan's attempt to relieve the crowded condition of her small islands. Whether or not things were really all that difficult for the Germans is a point for debate. Germany is probably in worse shape

195

for land today than she was in 1935, but today the Bonn government does not promote this as a problem. Nonetheless Professor Bilderback feels that in the early years of Hitler's power "large numbers of intelligent and humane persons 'believed' that the Eastern adventure was a matter of necessity for their own survival." The situation in Japan seems to me even more clear-cut. Crowding there seemed so serious to the people that, when their attempt to conquer additional territory failed, they instituted a drastic population control program.

There is every reason to believe that diminishing population pressures will reduce the probability of war, although it is difficult to predict how much of a reduction changing this single factor would produce. It is certainly clear that if population growth proceeds much further the probabilities of wars will be immensely increased.

CHAPTER 6

WHAT IF I'M WRONG?

Any scientist lives constantly with the possibility that he may be wrong. If he asks important questions, it is inevitable that some of the time he will come up with wrong answers. Many are caught before they see print; many are enshrined in the scientific literature. I've published a few myself, as some of my colleagues would gladly testify. Therefore it is important for you to consider that I, and many of the people who share my views, are just plain wrong, that we are alarmists, that technology or a miraculous change in human behavior or a totally unanticipated miracle in some other form will "save the day." Naturally, I find this highly unlikely; otherwise I would not have written this book. But the possibility must be considered.

To cover this contingency, I would like to propose an analogue to Pascal's famous wager. Pascal considered the only safe course for a man was to believe in God. If there was no God, it made no difference, but if there was, you ended up in heaven. In other words, play it safe. If I'm right, we will save the world. If I'm wrong, people will still be better fed, better housed, and happier, thanks to our efforts.

Will anything be lost if it turns out later that we can support a much larger population than seems possible today? Suppose we move to stabilize the size of the human population after the "time of famines" at two billion people, and we achieve that goal by 2050. Suppose that in 2051 someone invents a machine that will produce nutritious food or anything else man wants in limitless quantities out of nothing. Assume also that in 2051 mankind decides that the Earth is underpopulated with just two billion people. Men decide that they want more company. Fortunately, people can be produced in vast quantities by unskilled labor who enjoy their work. In about 500 years, with the proper encouragement of reproduction, the Earth could be populated to a density of about 100 individuals per square foot of surface (land and sea). That is a density that should please the loneliest person.

Remember, above all, that more than half of the world is in misery now. That alone should be enough to galvanize us into action, regardless of the exact dimensions of the future disaster now staring *Homo sapiens* in the face.

APPENDIX

What follows are the texts of letters that have
actually been sent to the addressees urging actions
related to the population problem.

Letter to a Member of the Protestant Clergy

Dr. Franklin Clark Fry, President
The Lutheran Church in America
231 Madison Avenue
New York, N.Y. 10016

Dear Dr. Fry:

As a concerned member of an L.C.A.
congregation, I feel compelled to draw
your attention, and that of all offi-
cers of the church, to the crises developing with our exploding human population.

It is noteworthy that in A Study Book

on the Manifesto, Dr. Pichaske cites several points from an address by Dr. Frank Zeidler, a political scientist. Among these are the following:

The ideological conflict between East and West has brought about... the loss of time and energy to solve such pressing problems as the population explosion.

The destructive use of our physical and personal resources has threatened our supplies of natural resources, polluted our water and air, and provided a major source for urban and rural distress.

What is even more noteworthy, and deeply tragic, is that Dr. Zeidler's address was cited only to show that modern man is in a time of change. And not to show that the church, corporately and individually, must take a stand to protect mankind from himself.

Two Sundays ago the Gospel text was the feeding of the five thousand. It would take a miracle of vastly greater proportions, continuing for years, to keep five hundred million people from starving to death in the next ten or fifteen years.

Some of them may be saved—if responsible population control measures are taken in the next few years. These would need to be measures which would reduce the worldwide (and that of each nation) birth rate to levels near or below the current death rate. Otherwise, the world food shortage (surpluses are essentially nonexistent now, as you are well aware) will be a major factor behind a catastrophic increase in the death rate. Five hundred million deaths is a reasonable guess only if the famine and pestilence finally stimulate the implementation of long-overdue measures.

Arguments purporting to show that mankind could meet the food needs of the world of, say, 1975 by increasing agricultural yield or farming the sea fail to consider current realities. Most arable land is already under intense (probably too intense) cultivation. Our environment is rapidly deteriorating, largely as a result of our crash programs to effect some short-term good, without considering long-term consequences. Further, we are not now farming the sea; we don't know what crops to grow in the sea. And even if we could determine that, we don't have the technology to farm it economically.

In view of these and many other considerations, it is imperative that the church take action. I would urge the Lutheran Church in America to begin to educate its members to several needs: the need for responsible parenthood (which is different from "planned parenthood"), the need for reduction and regulation of the birth rate, and the need for responsible programs in the worldwide activities of the church.

Sincerely,

John A. Hendrickson, Jr.

Letter from a Catholic Scientist to the Pope

His Holiness Pope Paul VI
Vatican City
Rome, Italy

Your Holiness:

I am writing to you as a concerned Catholic scientist. For some time now the ever-present problem of population increase has occupied a great deal of my attention. Your Holiness, there are too many people in the world today, and a decline in the birth rate does not seem to be occurring. There are no agricultural techniques that we have at present or that we will have at our disposal in the near enough future to avert a predicted massive famine. Famine will lead to war, and a large-scale war will seriously, if not permanently, shatter your hopes for world peace.

It is in consideration of the above that I am deeply troubled by your failure to act in a positive manner on the findings of your birth control commission. It would seem that the majority opinion of this commission, representing the views of the most competent theologians in the Church, has indicated that a change in the teaching of the Church with regard to birth control would be reasonable and consistent with the concept of development of doctrine that has so long been a part of our Christian tradition.

If there is any hope of preventing an irreparable disaster as a result of famine (in the near future), it will have to be through massive birth control programs, employing means of contraception other than periodic continence. It is for this reason that I strongly urge you to respond in a favorable manner to the majority opinion of your birth control commission.

Sincerely in Christ,

Dennis R. Parnell
NIH Postdoctoral Fellow

Letter from a Catholic Scientist to his Archbishop

Archbishop Joseph T. McGucken
441 Church Street
San Francisco, California 94114

Dear Archbishop McGucken:

The current controversy concerning Father John Maguire in the San Francisco Archdiocese points out very clearly, again, the unwillingness of the hierarchy of the Roman Catholic Church to be responsive to what is happening in the world and to do something about it.

In particular, the doctrines, dogmas, and pronouncements concerning the relationship between men and women need drastic revision and change. As the Church's teachings stand at present, they are a disgrace and a mockery and reflect neither Christian nor humanitarian ideals.

The Church must recognize all marriages as valid. The right to marry is the right of a man and a woman. The Church has assumed jurisdiction that does not belong to it.

The Church must encourage parents to have only as many children as they can care for—and parents must consider not only their own desires but the whole worldwide human population picture. The Church must affirm that the birth rate must soon be brought in line with the death rate—i.e., a growth rate of zero. This is the responsibility of all people regardless of race or religion.

The Church must recognize and state that all means of birth control are licit. Means of birth control are a medical problem.

Unfortunately, all marriages don't work. Divorce must be recognized by the Church and remarriage within it allowed. The present hypocrisy about Church annulments, dispensations, favors of the faith, etc., must stop.

The Church must put its concern for people, their welfare, and their happiness above its concern for doctrine, dogma, and canon law.

Many Roman Catholics already subscribe to my list of musts. It is time

that the Church stop being like a
reluctant little child, always needing
to be dragged into the present. Unless the Church changes, soon it will
come crashing down upon itself.

Sincerely,

John H. Thomas

Letter to the President of a Television Network

President, NBC Television Network
c/o KRON TV
San Francisco, California

Dear Sir:

I am extremely concerned about the
population crisis in the world as a
whole and as it affects the United
States. This is the most pressing
problem facing mankind; most of the
serious problems before us, such as
the pollution of our environment, our
urban problems, and even such political
difficulties as the war in Vietnam,
are all ultimately due to an overlarge
and still growing population. During
the next decade it is clear that
simply feeding this population will
make our present grave difficulties
seem like child's play.

The American public seems unaware of the gravity and imminence of the crisis, although some members of our government have become conscious of it. A few months ago Dean Rusk discussed it in a speech, equating it in importance with the Vietnam war. He was understating the case: the population explosion and its effects will be with us long after Vietnam is forgotten, but at least he recognizes it. President Johnson also mentioned it briefly in his State of the Union speech this year, as he has done before. He hopes to use modern communications techniques to reach the multiplying millions of Asia in a very imaginative way.

Apart from the daily press and some technical journals, the communications industry has done very little to awaken the public to the most serious problem it faces. There has been endless discussion of environment pollution, urban congestion, educational problems, unemployment, and poverty, but never a hint that overpopulation is a root cause. This country is getting crowded, but few suggest that perhaps the United States cannot or should not grow forever, or that continuous growth is not an unmixed blessing to our economy. If the problems are serious here in the United States, they are staggering on a world scale. Most other governments are aware of the problem, but they cannot solve it without our help.

The communications industry is in a unique and powerful position to inform and influence the public. Indeed, it has a responsibility to do so. There is much that can be done to make the public aware of the population explosion, of its impact on other problems, and even to encourage population control. There should be more discussions of the situation and possible means of dealing with it, including population control policies and methods for increasing food production. Further, the connection between our growing population and our increasing environmental and sociological problems must be made clear.

Much can be done indirectly. The problem can be dramatized through fiction. The advantages of small families can be emphasized in a variety of contexts. Women can be encouraged to find other interests besides children, and their husbands persuaded of the advantages of this. Birth control information, which has been well discussed, obviously should continue to be. Advertising and programming which cast large families in a favorable light should be strongly discouraged.

I hope you will give serious thought and support to policies of this sort in the future.

Sincerely yours,

Peter F. Brussard

Letter to a Senator

The Honorable George Murphy
United States Senate
Washington, D.C.

Dear Sir:

I am writing to you as a citizen who has been increasingly concerned about the grave problems facing our nation and the world, many of which are due to or at least aggravated by the "population explosion." The situation, which is apparently approaching a crisis condition in terms of worldwide food supplies, is a primary problem for the United States as well as the rest of the world. Indeed, if we do nothing or do no more than we are doing now, the situation is almost certainly hopeless.

There is a great deal that can and must be done on both foreign and domestic fronts. On the foreign side, besides sending food to those who need it, we must vastly increase our aid to improve food production locally in underdeveloped countries. Such aid must be tied to strong population control programs. Both kinds of programs are absolutely essential if underdeveloped countries are to become self-sufficient.

Domestically, there is also much to be done. Our own population growth must be stopped if we are to solve such environmental problems as various kinds of pollution, and urban congestion, and our social ills, such as poverty, unemployment, and rising crime rates—all of these traceable at least in part to overpopulation. Furthermore, we cannot hope or expect to convince the rest of the world to stop multiplying if we do not.

I strongly urge you to give serious consideration and support to any program that will encourage our population to stop growing, whether in the form of changes in the law or changes in our welfare and social programs, and I urge you to support any policies that give positive assistance to the rest of the world in stopping population growth and increasing food production.

> Very sincerely,
>
> Dorothy W. Decker
> (Mrs. Harry A. Decker)

Letter to a Member of the House of Representatives

The Honorable Charles S. Gubser
House of Representatives
Washington, D.C.

Dear Sir:

I am writing to you as a resident of the San Francisco Bay Area who is deeply concerned about the exploding population—both in the world in general and as illustrated by problems in the Bay Area in particular.

The ills of overpopulation are obvious in the Bay Area: increasing smog, water pollution (especially in the Bay), water shortages, and suburbia and concrete spreading across irreplaceable orchard land. All this is aside from the traffic congestion, the noise, the rising crime rates, the riots—all the usual social symptoms of the overcrowding of people.

I feel that it is time to stop encouraging new industry and new people to come to California—time to stop hailing all expansion as "progress." I strongly object to the filling of the Bay—not only because of the earthquake hazard on such manufactured land, but also because it is altering our climate for the worse and destroying a prime natural resource and recreational facility—all to make room for more people.

I believe that overpopulation is the most important issue facing the world today and that the United States as a world leader should be doing everything in her power to meet it. Starvation is a fact of life in many areas of the world right now and will be worse tomorrow. Every incident of unrest around the world can be traced at least in part to overpopulation— and as the pressures from increased population heighten, so will the unrest. Surely there is no more serious problem.

I strongly urge you to give your serious consideration and support to all efforts, domestic and foreign, that seek to establish <u>effective</u> population control.

                    Very sincerely,

                    Ann W. Duffield
                    (Mrs. Wendell A. Duffield)

FOOTNOTES

1. Since this was written, 1968 figures have appeared, showing that the doubling time is now 35 years.
2. J. H. Fremlin, "How Many People Can the World Support?" *New Scientist*, October 29, 1964.
3. To understand this, simply consider what would happen if we held the population constant at three billion people by exporting all the surplus people. If this were done for 37 years (the time it now takes for one doubling) we would have exported three billion people—enough to populate a twin planet of the Earth to the same density. In two doubling times (74 years) we would reach a total human population for the solar system of 12 billion people, enough to populate the Earth and three similar planets to the density found on Earth today. Since the areas of the planets and moons mentioned above are not three times that of the Earth, they can be populated to equal density in much less than two doubling times.
4. "Interstellar Migration and the Population Problem." *Heredity* 50: 68–70, 1959.
5. I. J. Cook, *New Scientist*, September 8, 1966
6. The birth rate is more precisely the total number of births in a country during a year, divided by the total population at the midpoint of the year, multiplied by 1,000. Suppose that there were 80 births in Lower Slobbovia during 1967, and that the population of Lower Slobbovia was 2,000 on July 1, 1967. Then the birth rate would be:

Birth rate $= \dfrac{80 \text{ (total births in L. Slobbovia in 1967)}}{2,000 \text{ (total population, July 1, 1967)}} \times 1,000$

$= .04 \times 1,000 = 40$

Similarly if there were 40 deaths in Lower Slobbovia during 1967, the death rate would be:

Death rate $= \dfrac{40 \text{ (total deaths in L. Slobbovia in 1967)}}{2,000 \text{ (total population, July 1, 1967)}} \times 1,000$

$= .02 \times 1,000 = 20$

Then the Lower Slobbovian birth rate would be 40 per thousand, and the death rate would be 20 per thousand. For every 1,000 Lower Slobbovians alive on July 1, 1967, 40 babies were born and 20 people died. Subtracting the death rate from the birth rate gives us the rate of natural increase of Lower Slobbovia for the year 1967. That is, 40 − 20 = 20; during 1967 the population grew at a rate of 20 people per thousand per year. Dividing that rate by ten expresses the increase as a percent (the increase per hundred per year). The increase in 1967 in Lower Slobbovia was two percent. Remember that this rate of increase ignores any movement of people into and out of Lower Slobbovia.

7. McGraw-Hill Book Company, Inc., New York. 1965.

8. Human brain size increased from an apelike capacity of about 500 cubic centimeters (cc) in *Australopithecus* to about 1,500 cc in modern *Homo sapiens*. Among modern men small variations in brain size do not seem to be related to significant differences in the ability to use cultural information, and there is no particular reason to believe that our brain size will continue to increase. Further evolution may occur more readily in a direction of increased efficiency rather than increased size.

9. This is, of course, an oversimplified explanation. For more detail see Ehrlich and Holm, *The Process of Evolution*, McGraw-Hill Book Company, Inc., New York. 1963.

10. These data and those that follow on the decline of death rates are from Kingsley Davis's "The Amazing Decline of Mortality in Underdeveloped Areas," *The American Economic Review*, Vol. 46, pp. 305–318.

11. August 7, 1965.

12. *Look,* March 7, 1967.

13. W. and P. Paddock, *Famine—1975!,* Little, Brown & Co., Boston.

14. Addressing the Synthetic Organic Chemical Manufacturers Association of the United States, November 9, 1967.

15. Washington, D.C., February 20, 1968.

16. Professor of Pharmacology, Stanford University School of Medicine, speaking to the Palo Alto Kiwanis Club, January 25, 1968.

17. Houghton Mifflin Co., Boston. 1968.

18. Address to the American Association for the Advancement of Science, December 27, 1967.

19. G. M. Woodwell, "Toxic Substances and Ecological Cycles," *Scientific American,* March, 1967.

20. *BioScience,* January, 1968.

21. Address to the AAAS, December 27, 1967.

22. C. F. Wurster, Jr., "DDT Reduces Photosynthesis by Marine Phytoplankton," *Science* 159: 1474–1475.

23. "Lead Poisoning and the Fall of Rome," *Journal of Occupational Medicine* 7: 53–60, 1965.

24. "Criteria for an Optimum Human Environment." 1967 Manuscript.

25. "Population Policy: Will Current Programs Succeed?", November 10, 1967.

26. "It's God's Will. Why Interfere?", *The New York Times Magazine,* January 14, 1968.

27. *New Scientist,* July 27, 1967.

28. *The Atlantic Monthly,* December, 1967.

29. February 23, 1968.

30. January 28, 1967, p. 86.

31. *Scientific American,* November 1964, p. 99.

32. *Famine—1975!,* p. 66.

33. Address to the Second International Conference on War on Hunger.

34. "Phytopathology in a Hungry World," *Ann. Rev. Phytopath.* Vol. 5, 375–390. 1967.
35. Dial Press, New York. 1967, p. 161.
36. "Mass Insect Control Programs: Four Case Histories." *Psyche* 68: 75–111; 1961.
37. M. Evans and Co., Inc., New York. 1966.
38. *see* C. Cottam, *BioScience,* July 1965, pp. 458–459, for summary and documentation.
39. Page 123.
40. Hearings before the Subcommittee on Foreign Aid Expenditures of the Committee on Government Operations, United States Senate, Eighty-ninth Congress. Second Session on S. 1676.
41. Part 2-b, August 24, 1965.
42. July 9, 1965.
43. *Moment in the Sun,* Dial Press, Inc., N. Y., p. 3.
44. *Commercial and Financial Chronicle,* August 11, 1966.
45. Quoted by LaMonte Cole, loc. cit.
46. *Scientist and Citizen,* November-December, 1967.
47. *The Great Frontier,* Houghton Mifflin Co., Boston. 1952.
48. Vol. 155, March 10, 1967.
49. Dr. Henderson has just received an extremely favorable reply to his letter. The Board of Social Ministry of the Lutheran Church in America has a highly enlightened policy on population. It is unfortunate that this church's stand is not more widely known.

BIBLIOGRAPHY

I am listing here a series of books of general interest on the population-food-environment situation. These sources will also provide entry to the general literature of the field.

Appleman Philip. 1965, 1966. *The Silent Explosion*. Beacon Press, Boston.

Borgstrom Georg. 1967. *The Hungry Planet*. Collier Books, New York. Collier-Macmillan Ltd., London.

Carson, Rachel. 1962. *Silent Spring*. Houghton Mifflin Co., Boston.

Commoner Barry. 1967. *Science and Survival*. Viking Pres Inc., New York.

Day, Lincoln H., and Alice Taylor Day. 1965. *Too Many Americans*. Delta Press, Inc., New York.

DeBach Paul (ed.). 1964. *Biological Control of Insect Pests and Weeds*. Lienhold Publishing Corp., New York

Ehrlich, Paul R., and Richard W. Holm, 1963. *The Process of Evolution*. McGraw-Hill Book Company, Inc., New York.

Graham, Frank. 1966. *Disaster by Default: Politics and Water Pollution*. M. Evans & Co., New York.

218

Bibliography

Hardin, Garrett (ed.). *Population, Evolution and Birth Control*. W. H. Freeman & Co., San Francisco and London.

Hauser, Philip M. 1963. *The Population Dilemma*. Prentice-Hall, Inc., Englewood Cliffs, New Jersey.

Herber, Lewis. 1962. *Our Synthetic Environment*. Alfred A. Knopf, Inc., New York.

Hopcraft, Arthur. 1968. *Born to Hunger*. Houghton Mifflin Co., Boston.

Lader, Lawrence. 1966. *Abortion*. Beacon Press, Boston.

Loraine, John A., and E. Trevor Bell. 1968. *Fertility and Contraception in the Human Female*. E. & S. Livingstone Ltd., Edinburgh and London.

Lowe, David. 1966. *Abortion and the Law*. Pocket Books, New York.

Maury, Marian (ed.). 1963. *Birth Rate and Birth Right*. Macfadden-Bartell Corp., New York.

The Next Ninety Years. Proceedings of a Conference sponsored by the Office for Industrial Associates at the California Institute of Technology. March 7-8, 1967. California Institute of Technology, Pasadena.

Ng, Larry K. Y., and Stuart Mudd (eds.). 1965. *The Population Crisis*. Indiana University Press, Bloomington and London.

Osborn, Fairfield. 1948. *Our Plundered Planet*. Little, Brown & Co., Boston, Toronto.

Paddock, William and Paul Paddock. 1964. *Hungry Nations*. Little, Brown & Co., Boston, Toronto.

Paddock, William and Paul Paddock. 1967. *Famine —1975!* Little, Brown & Co., Boston, Toronto.

Population Bulletin. Population Reference Bureau, Inc. 1755 Massachusetts Avenue, N.W., Washington, D.C. 20036.

Reinow, Robert, and Leona Train Reinow. 1967. *Moment in the Sun*. Dial Press, Inc., New York.

Rudd, Robert L. 1966. *Pesticides and the Living Landscape*. University of Wisconsin Press, Madison, Milwaukee, London.

Sax, Karl. 1955, 1960. *Standing Room Only, The World's Exploding Population*. Beacon Press, Boston.

Thompson, Warren S., and David T. Lewis. 1965. *Population Problems*. 5th ed. McGraw-Hill Book Company, Inc., New York.

ACKNOWLEDGMENTS

First and foremost I am indebted to my colleagues in the Population Biology Group, Department of Biological Sciences, Stanford University. They have spent many hours discussing the population problem with me and have made many helpful suggestions. The following have taken the time to read and comment upon the entire manuscript: David M. Bell, Peter F. Brussard, Valerie C. Chase, Lawrence E. Gilbert, Jr., John A. Hendrickson, Jr., Richard W. Holm, Andrew R. Moldenke, Dennis R. Parnell, Peter H. Raven, Margaret A. Sharp, Michael C. Singer, and John H. Thomas. I have been associated with Professors Holm, Raven, and Thomas in work on the "population explosion" for many years. Much of their thinking is incorporated in this book—I have shamelessly pirated their ideas without crediting them individually. In spite of this they have been kind enough to endorse the ideas expressed.

Professor Donald Kennedy, Executive Head of the Department of Biological Sciences at Stanford, has also read the manuscript, wielded his fine editorial pen over it, and expressed his endorsement of its contents. Professor Jonathan L. Freedman of Stanford's Department of Psychology has also reviewed the

221

manuscript and has been especially helpful in discussing problems of crowding. Other colleagues have read the manuscript or helped me in other ways. In Stanford's Medical School these include Dr. John W. Farquhar (Department of Medicine), Dr. H. Russel Hulett (Department of Genetics), Dr. Sumner M. Kalman (Department of Pharmacology), and Dr. Sidney Liebes, Jr. (Department of Genetics). Professor Loy Bilderback of the Department of History, Fresno State College, Professor Kenneth E. F. Watt of the Department of Zoology, University of California at Davis, and Professor Joseph H. Camin of the Department of Entomology, University of Kansas, in addition to reading the manuscript, have discussed problems related to the book with me in great detail. Many of their ideas have been included. Many colleagues at other institutions have encouraged me both in person and by mail, and the fact that I cannot list them does not indicate a lack of appreciation. My intellectual debt to the many writers on this subject who have preceded me should be obvious from the references and bibliography.

My attorney, Johnson C. Montgomery, has had a long-term interest in the causes and cures of the population explosion, and we have spent a great deal of time together conferring on various aspects of the problem. He and his wife, Nancy Riva Montgomery, have both read the manuscript critically. Their assistance and ideas have been invaluable. I am also grateful to Mrs. Harry A. Decker, Mrs. Wendell A. Duffield, and Mrs. Lawrence E. Gilbert, Jr., for their aid in preparing the manuscript and for their suggestions for its improvement.